The Occult, Magic & Witchcraft

The Occult, Magic & Witchcraft

An exploration of modern sorcery

Charles W. Olliver

This edition published in 2022 by Arcturus Publishing Limited
26/27 Bickels Yard, 151–153 Bermondsey Street,
London SE1 3HA

This book was originally published in 1928 under the title *A Handbook of Magic &
Witchcraft*.

Typeset by Couper Street.
Images are in the public domain.

AD008789UK

Printed in the UK

CONTENTS

AUTHOR'S PREFACE

The introductory chapter of the present volume gives a sufficient idea of the scope of the work, and of the author's object in writing it. Wherever quotations have been made, references are given, and a complete bibliography of the books referred to by the author is appended.

The author wishes to extend his thanks to all who have helped him, and particularly to the Director of the British Museum for permission to examine certain lesser known books, to his friends A. K. Das and J. K. Taylor for assistance in proof-reading and other matters, and to his friend H. Thurley, who read the manuscript in its original form, and for whose suggestions he is very grateful.

C. W. OLLIVER.

London, 1928.

INTRODUCTION

The life of Charles Wolfran Olliver is as mysterious as the subject of this book of essays. We know that he was a British writer who was born in 1895 and wrote all his works in the first half of the 20th century. He studied at the Ecole Superieure d'Electricitée in Paris and had enough of an interest in electrical engineering to write a book called *The AC Commutator Motor* in 1927. Olliver was in thrall to science and scientific enquiry and this book, published a year later, under the title *A Handbook of Magic and Witchcraft*, sought to bring a scientific rigour to the study of these subjects. This was not a wholly unusual occurrence in intellectuals of the late 19th and early 20th century. The Society for Psychical Research, which Olliver mentions in his introduction, produced bound volumes of their investigations into seances and Spiritualists. The American Spiritualist movement was wildly popular at that time and so the split between those interested in the natural world and those interested in the supernatural was not as pronounced as it is in our times. There was a supposition that there was a science behind explained phenomena and it merely needed to be uncovered.

An proponent of this idea was the Nobel Laureate Charles Richet (1850-1935), who won the 'Prize for Physiology or Medicine' in 1913 for his discoveries around anaphylaxis. This decorated scientist was of the opinion that all paranormal phenomena was down to a sense that science hadn't yet pinned down. *'It has been shown that as regards subjective metapsychics the simplest and most rational explanation is to suppose the existence of a faculty of supernormal cognition... setting in motion the human intelligence by certain vibrations that do not move the normal senses.'*

Clearly much taken by the work of Charles Richet, Olliver attempted to build on his theories. In 1932 he wrote *The Extension of Consciousness: An Introduction to the Study of Metapsychology* which was a continuation of his research into the work of Richet. This work covered cryptaesthesia (extrasensory perception such as clairvoyance or clairaudience) telekinesis and materialization. Richet appears to have had a dramatic impact on Olliver and he was impressed by his investigations into various mediums of the age. The problem is that Richet appears to have been a very credulous investigator and was even duped by Joaquín Argamasilla, who Harry Houdini exposed as a fraud in 1924. While Richet's medical achievements are not in any doubt, his reputation as a professor of physiology bolstered his decidedly shoddy work on the supernatural.

In *A Handbook of Magic and Witchcraft* some of the subjects Richet investigated are covered, but the aim appears to be more linking religious sentiment to what Olliver called the Devil-Myth, sex magic, and other paranormal phenomena. He uses definitions that are contemporary to his time and naturally uses dated, unconsciously biased terms such as 'black magic' and 'white magic'.

Depressingly, he also subscribes to his admired Richet's view of the intelligence of different races. Charles Richet was a eugenicist who was well known to hold racist views on the hierarchy of intelligence among different peoples of the world and Olliver follows in his footsteps in saying that Aborigine Australians 'are the least developed race of men'. He attempts to give as his reasoning for this obnoxious view the incorrect supposition that some Aborigine tribes in Australia don't know the connection between sex and childbirth. This was down to flawed research by anthropologists in the late 1920s. Such ridiculous ideas can only find fertile ground in a society that routinely discriminated against those without white European ancestry.

This present abridged edition has left in some of this objectionable material so that the author's arguments can be understood within the context of his wider views on race, sex and society. However, where clarity is needed, some minor changes, cuts and additions have been made. For example, in places, 'black magic' has been replaced with 'magic with evil intent'. On occasion, the word 'man' to denote 'human' has been replaced with that word to avoid confusion when talking about phallic worship and to differentiate more easily between the gender and the species. Beyond these edits for clarity, the work is of its time and is a fascinating look at what happens when you apply scientific dogma to subjects beyond the usual ken of science.

CHAPTER I

INTRODUCTORY

The sub-title of these essays – *A Retrospective Introduction to the Study of Modern Metapsychics* – is more or less self-explanatory, the present introduction being written in order that the reader may have a comprehensive idea of the object and general aims of the work, the plan on which it is written, and, above all, a clear idea of the terminology used throughout and the classification that I have attempted to introduce.

The subject is so vast, and moreover the tributary subjects so numerous, that I have had to adhere rigidly to an inflexible line throughout; the present volume is itself intended as an introduction to a more complete treatise, and should be considered as such. The reader will not find in these essays anything beyond an attempt at a classification of facts. The description and demonstration of these I have in some places given, reducing the examples as far as possible by choosing those that seemed to have the most direct bearing on the case, or the circumstances attending which seemed more conclusive and typical. It should be clearly understood that these examples are not isolated cases, but are taken from hundreds of similar occurrences.

It is of course, impossible within the scope of a work such as this to give anything like the number of facts necessary properly to substantiate the statements made. Any attempt at this would run to several volumes, and would undoubtedly impair that conciseness and clarity which are indispensable if the reader is to gain a comprehensive insight of the subject as a whole.

In every case, however, the necessary references have been given and a bibliography is appended which, though not complete, does contain those works in which the reader will find descriptions and innumerable examples to substantiate the facts which the author has in most cases been forced by space to merely state as such.

Writers at all times have found a rich mine to exploit, and an endless source of inspiration in the lore and legends of the past, and more particularly in the mysterious beliefs and strange events connected with what is commonly known as magic and witchcraft.

The belief in another world, in ghosts and hauntings, in some secret and awful power wielded for good or evil by magicians and sorcerers has always appealed to human nature and is one of the most persistent heirlooms of the past, traceable to the fearsome creeds and corrupted demonologies of the origin of religions.

Phenomena that are now explained and classified, and the incipient efforts of scientific control gave mankind the necessary foundation for such beliefs; legends elaborated by generations of priest-rulers did the rest.

The astonishing revival of witchcraft and black magic in the Middle Ages gave new life to superstitions and beliefs that might well otherwise have died out long before our time, and the taint and influence of this dark chapter in the world's history can be felt acutely to this day in the whole of the world.

A sentence for sorcery was passed against a shepherd in France as late as 1858 and, in January 1926, at Melun, a case of sorcery was again brought before the courts, such cases being comparatively common among the peasantry of most countries.

Beliefs and superstitions that are deeply rooted in the minds of peasants are latent in the minds of a great number of civilised and educated men today, and are constantly being stirred into some semblance of reality by accounts the very vagueness of which serves only to encourage wonder and speculation.

Apart from these various reasons, some of us, during the course of our lives, have experiences which we are quite at a loss to explain; this may take the more usual form of a monition, or the rarer form of an apparition, in either case it reopens the whole question of occultism and superstition. Leaving aside the ever-present mystery of human life and its ultimate destiny, if once one begins to admit any of the facts that are so improperly called supernatural, he is immediately faced with the hopelessly intricate and involved problems of magic and witchcraft.

There is a further and far more important cause for speculation at the present time. Ever since the appearance of the Sisters Fox in 1847, and even of Mesmer in 1778, new and strange phenomena have been brought to general notice. Mesmerism has to a great extent been taken up as a practical science and adapted to medical uses, and as such probably holds little place in the speculations of the average man on the occult; but the same cannot be said of spiritualism, which from its very start in America has laid the whole problem once again before the human mind in a different form.

From its original simple manifestations spiritualism developed rapidly into a bewildering collection of phenomena; raps and table-turning, revelations from beyond, accounts of conversations with departed great men, apparitions and monitions became so numerous as to be almost banal; spiritualism became a mode; mediums gifted with mediocre powers had recourse to arrant trickery, while innumerable others arose who had not even some original power to give as an excuse for deceit.

Seances were given and repeated all over Europe and America, the Society for Psychical Research and others filled volumes with accounts and anecdotes relating to occult phenomena, the outstanding feature of which seems to have been the utter lack of any kind of protection against fraud, and the total absence of scientific observation. And so spiritualism gained and spread, hopelessly tainted from its very birth by fraud and hysteria, till it was everywhere an object of derision which no sane scientific mind could even consider.

To make matters worse, spiritualism became a religion, and those who practised it with any degree of sincerity immediately lost the faculty of scientific observation. Throughout the world's history this tendency to consider as a religion, good or evil, any phenomena pertaining to the occult, has been the greatest stumbling-block in the way of the investigator and, in the case of spiritualism, it is hard to say which, of the frauds of so-called mediums, or the blind credulity of religious adepts, has done the greater harm to the cause of science, or put more obstacles in the way towards finding the true explanation of the phenomena in question.

However, deep under all the apparent fraud and insincerity of spiritualism, scientific thinkers began to realise that there was some foundation of truth, and although no sane man could believe that the shade of Napoleon or Pythagoras would return to some suburban parlour to converse with local enthusiasts, yet the mass of collected observations, when carefully sifted and examined, seemed to leave behind some residue of truth and fact.

Moreover, certain exceptional mediums such as Stanton Moses, Holme, Eusapia Paladino, and others were kept away from ordinary public seances and carefully studied and examined by medical and scientific experts with a view to settling once and for all the possibility, or otherwise, of occult phenomena.

For years patient and thorough investigators devoted their energies to this till at last in 1923 a well-known French scientist, Professor Charles Richet, in his *Traité de Metapsychique*, gave the world a book in which, through years of patient labour during which he collected and verified countless cases, he clearly and finally demonstrated the existence of three types of phenomena unknown to ordinary science, thus laying the foundation of a new science, the science of intelligent forces, or science of Metapsychics.

The great merit of Professor Charles Richet's book is that he does not in any way attempt to explain. He admits freely that he does not know. It was an obvious absurdity to elaborate complex theories for the explanation of phenomena the very existence of which was highly doubtful, and indeed denied by the great majority. The first step was to give definite and irrefutable proof that such facts existed, after which, perhaps, when these had been thoroughly and repeatedly examined, some working theory at least might be evolved and tested. This demonstration Professor Richet has achieved.

After reading his book there is but little room for doubt. The extraordinary care with which the experiments were conducted, the elaborate precautions which were taken to eliminate the remotest possibility of fraud, the scientific qualifications of those engaged in the investigations all form an argument which cannot be lightly put aside.

Professor Richet has opened a new era in the history of the occult; although the immense importance of his work is not as yet fully realised, he has laid the foundation stone of a new science the significance of which cannot be ignored.

Professor Richet very rightly considers only such cases as have come under his immediate control; his object is demonstration, and in such a book there is no room for anything that cannot be corroborated in every detail. Other phenomena, other cases dealing with identical or similar phenomena he cites as interesting collateral evidence, but his arguments rest only on such facts as are beyond doubt or speculation.

His subject is in itself so vast and intricate, the material which he had to sift so abundant and complex that he has had to restrict himself to modern times. Besides, the investigator who turns to the past finds himself faced with legend and superstition, with science in its infancy, with elaborate philosophical systems, and no scientific demonstration can be based on such data, distorted as it is by credulity and tradition.

The fact remains, however, that at the present day, in the twentieth century, in spite of the wonderful progress of science, the existence has been proved of facts utterly unlike anything to be found within the domain of science proper. There is every reason to believe that patient investigation of these new phenomena will lead to unsuspected discoveries, and the interest that must arise once more reopens the whole question of occult science.

It becomes immediately apparent that the lore of the past, that magic and witchcraft, that the thousand beliefs and superstitions that have accumulated and developed since the very dawn of civilisation, when examined in the light of this new science, may possibly reveal their few remaining secrets.

It is the object of this book to dispel the mystery and superstitious horror which surround the fallacies of the past, to show up sorcery in its true light, to reduce magic to its proper relative importance, and show that all these beliefs and doctrines were but normal phases in the evolution and elaboration of the human mind. Some of these so-called mysteries can be attributed to religious influences, some to science proper, some to crime and insanity, and others finally to such phenomena as have been rediscovered and demonstrated within recent times under the name of metapsychics.

While it is my object to explain the origin of magic and witchcraft, and therefore necessarily to examine the origin and growth of religious systems, it should be remembered that we are dealing with facts. I must leave all considerations as to the relative truth or merits of various beliefs and religions entirely aside.

I only consider and study religion in these essays as being the most important factor in the history of human thought, and as the common origin and cradle of all those strange beliefs that have amalgamated to form what is known as the occult.

As we look back over the past ages and try and unravel the tangled web of religious belief we invariably find that we have at the origin of all creeds deification of nature in some form or other, and also the supposition of some universal Being or God either derive from natural demonology, or pre-existing, in which latter case the demonology is derived from a philosophical idea of God, whereas in the first case an abstract idea of God is elaborated from natural demonology at a later date, as civilisation proceeds. This universal Being or Spirit is usually derived from a particular case of nature worship, sometimes that of fire as being to primitive beings the phenomenon most nearly akin to the spiritual.

At some period the theory or secret of life, which is to be found universally in all religions and philosophical systems as a symbol or condensed expression of the three and fourfold mystery, makes its appearance, and this essentially simple creed may be taken as the origin and foundation of all symbols and initiatic rites. Briefly stated, it consists of the conception of the unity or Spirit, the existence of which presupposes the necessary existence of matter or duality, which in turn entails the existence of a bond or relation between the two, thus forming a trinity.

We shall show in later chapters how important a part this original creed played in the religious and mystic history of the world, and how every form of worship and belief and consequent symbol can be traced back to misconceptions and misinterpretations of this original axiom. The mysterious

trinities that are to be found in all religions have no other
origin, and the pillars of the Temple of Solomon with their
cross-stone had no other meaning. One of the earliest and
most important misinterpretations of this symbol gave rise to
sex worship, and thus we find that the apparent origin of most
religions and religious ceremonies is sexual. Moreover, the
whole nature of life and the 'lure of the flesh' were such that
this second meaning of the universal symbol, that pertaining
to material life, was the nearest to primitive people evolving
new religions, and therefore the most likely to be adopted.
The confusion arose from the idea of creating life, which was
taken as meaning the creation of human or living beings, and
this being the attribute of humanity that most undoubtedly
seemed to primitive man to be similar or nearest to God,
the Creator of all things, was very naturally considered as
being the alpha and omega of life. It served the purpose of the
priests most admirably to let the sex delusion spread among
the people and so sex worship arose in its crude original form.

Another reason for this, and a very important one, was
that the life of a nation in uncivilised times, its power and
riches, depended entirely on its having as dense a population
as possible. Hence the worship of the creative function
served a threefold purpose: it was blind to the true meaning
of religion which thus retained its power as a mysterious
initiation; it was a popular worship for the people; it
increased the population and thus strengthened the tribe
against its enemies and neighbours.

Meanwhile, the pre-existing demonology was incorporated
in the form of minor gods or, if no such worship pre-existed,
then it was evolved later, as the natural tendency of

mankind was to endow with spirit intelligence those natural phenomena which it was unable to understand. In this way we get the synthesis of all religious systems in their cruder form, and so they progressed. There came a time, however, when civilisation and gentler customs made open phallic worship difficult, if not impossible. Such a crude form of worship could not be accepted literally by more enlightened beings, and philosophers the world over were elaborating systems where the 'spirit' played a predominant part. Thus do we get early forms of that philosophy which from Buddha through Plato to Schopenhauer has always been discussed and elaborated in every country from the earliest days to the present time, but which through the sterile speculations and hair-splitting sophistry of most of its supporters has always missed the point by either going too far or not far enough. Such doctrines taken literally in their true form were only adhered to by the very few, the more advanced and higher intellects, and never found favour with the majority. In the meantime, something had to be done for humanity as a whole.

As we have seen, the cruder forms of phallic worship were rapidly becoming impracticable, and if the priests were to retain their dignity and power, some new form of worship had to be elaborated that would be more in keeping with the times.

Thus at this period we find the phallic worship as such fading away and the cruder representations of it replaced by symbols, which become less and less plain and obvious till even the sexual meaning of these disappeared, as it has in modern times when few indeed are those who realise that the gods they worship and the forms of their cult and ritual are of purely phallic origin.

But this transformation did not take place all at once. The idea of a God such as the Hebrew God was brought in gradually, divine revelations were invented wholesale, such philosophers as Buddha were 'deified' and declared to have had no beginning and to have no end, the demons and spirits of former natural demonologies became minor gods or saints, and the heterogeneous whole was woven together with complicated legends, similar the world over, and all of them based on parables and symbolism, the inner meaning of which, of course, was always the story of procreation and gestation or the cycle of life. The Sun having been taken from the earliest times as the prototype in the heavens of life on earth, its rising and setting compared to birth and death, and the seasons corresponding to youth and age, it followed that from the teachings of astronomy, the very earliest of all sciences, a whole theurgic system was propounded from the heavens, and this again was mixed into the religious melting pot.

It is hardly to be wondered at that it should be difficult to find a clue to the tangled web of religious origins, the more so when we consider the inter-reactions of various nations and creeds among one another and consequent further complication. In trying to unravel this problem investigators came to one or other of two blind alleys, sex, or natural demonology, and to that stone wall there was no apparent opening.

Meanwhile, that wonderful conglomeration of primitive beliefs and legends took a firm hold on the world's history. Those with ambitious schemes were not slow to realise the possibilities of religion. On account of its inherent complication and the vagueness and multiplicity of its origins, religion became a nest of dissension and an excuse for political ambition. Thus through the consequent political and religious upheavals, the schisms, heresies and abuses of every kind, the massacres and persecutions, the history of religion was written, a tale of blood and unwarrantable violence. Reformers arose, extremists on account of the very corruption they were out to abolish, and thus again religion became more involved, and narrower in its outlook. The dogmas of the various sects or divisions became mere questions of irrelevant detail.

Through all this there had always been some vague hidden tradition of the original starting point. Sorcery, and the witches' sabbat of the Middle Ages have always been attributed to a corruption of magic, although it is a significant fact that no trace can be found in those times of flourishing sorcery of anything resembling true magic, the initiates of which were men of too pure motives and too advanced views to vulgarise their creed or reveal in any way the secrets of a science they only partially understood. Sorcery can be traced to the fear and superstition of the Middle Ages and more ignorant civilisations when all things were endowed with demons and spirits, and hence, anyone having even a slight knowledge of any form of science such as physics, chemistry, or medicine would be naturally regarded with awe, and as one commanding spirits. That in order to do this he must have signed a pact with the evil one, king of the spirits of darkness, was a foregone conclusion. It must be remembered that the Church, and the Church alone, was responsible for the creation of the Devil-Myth, no trace of this existing in the earlier forms of demonology.

If this is sufficient to explain sorcery as the unhealthy and fear-begotten speculations of the uneducated on the mass of involved legends and superstitions, coupled with a knowledge of poisons and rudimentary science and a strong disposition for crime and perversion, it is not to this source that we can trace the more obnoxious practices of the witches' sabbat, actual Devil-worship, and magic with evil intent. Each of these will be studied in a special chapter, and it will be shown that the sabbats were corruptions of religious rituals by sects who were slowly reverting to the original phallic worship, and who, through analogy with sorcerers and witches amalgamated with these for the joint purpose of sexual excess and crime. There is in fact nothing strange in this; it is merely a reversion to old religious rites, modified often beyond recognition by the follies of overwrought and drug-sodden imaginations, but nevertheless religion identical with its early forms. The sabbat, if we remove its characteristic Devil-worship and appended sorcery, has existed in identically the same form from the earliest times through the Bacchanalia, Saturnalia, and Floralia of the Greeks and Romans, right to modem times.

The sabbats were merely a particularly corrupt and obnoxious episode in the history of these phallic mani-festations, due to the sorcery and devil-infested atmosphere of the Middle Ages. They neither arose suddenly in the Middle Ages nor died out afterwards, they are merely a link in the long chain of religious phallus-worshipping sects.

We see therefore that the history of magic and witchcraft is intimately connected with the growth and development of religion, and I have in consequence found it necessary to devote a chapter to the dawn of religions. Humans ever since primitive times have had an irresistible tendency to worship what they could not understand and explain, hence such mysterious phenomena as are connected with sorcery or magic and with the early manifestations of metapsychics are intermixed with religion and the various cults and worships of dissident sects.

The general plan I have followed in these essays can be stated as follows. An examination of the origin of religious beliefs and an outline of their growth and development form the opening chapter. The true and final origin of religion is a subject that has led and still leads to much speculation. It is undoubtedly manifold, and ignorant as we are still of the origin of our kind and of the dawn of intelligent thought, we have little or no material at our disposal. But there is no necessity for the purpose of tracing sorcery and magic to go back to the origins of human thought. Moreover, the extraordinary similarity, one might almost say identity, of beliefs and the fundamental principles of all religions throughout the world leave us little room for doubt or misinterpretation. Certain modern writers have elaborately proved and brought to light the sexual origin of cults and ceremonies. They have not gone far enough. The sexual phase of religious development is of paramount importance, and practically universal, but it is not the origin of the religious systems of the present day, nor is the phallic explanation of religious symbolism correct. The trinitarian creed that I have mentioned was the true origin of all symbols and doctrines, and two misinterpretations of this symbol led to phallic worship and the Devil-Myth, the most important factors in religious evolution and the main causes to be found at the root of sorcery and magic with evil intent. The two chapters following on that concerning the dawn of religions deal, the first with phallic worship, the second with the Devil-Myth, and are the natural conclusion of the chapter on religious origins, leading to the chapters on sorcery, the sabbat and magic with good intent.

It is necessary here that I should define the terminology I have used throughout these essays so that there may be no ambiguity in the reader's mind concerning the meaning of the various terms used. As regards the past, I have called Demonology the endowment by human beings of certain phenomena with God or spirit personalities. By natural demonology I mean those demonological systems which are more directly derived from natural phenomena.

The terms 'Magic and Sorcery', 'Witchcraft' and 'Black Magic' have been indiscriminately and quite improperly used, and this has given rise to considerable confusion. I have grouped under the heading of Sorcery such practices as were derived from misguided and incomplete scientific knowledge coupled with superstitious rites, but with a very decided taint of crime and sexual perversion.

Under the heading of 'White Magic' I have grouped those carefully hidden initiations which have existed within religious systems at all times, and have existed simultaneously within various secret societies handed down from generation to generation or adept to adept by tradition. The secrets of complete initiation were, of course, supposed to endow the possessor with certain strange powers which we shall later analyse and examine. In most cases the secret societies quite early lost the true meaning of their fundamental symbols, and the mere shell remains. Magic as I have defined it may seem to the reader to be taken in a very narrow sense, but I wish to point out that it is the true sense, and that the greater portion of phenomena usually grouped under the heading of 'Magic' have nothing whatever in common with the doctrine of initiates but should be classified under the heading of 'Sorcery' or even of 'Black Magic'.

Black Magic is an entity in itself, partaking both of sorcery, to which it is most nearly akin, and of magic. It can be defined as a corruption and total misinterpretation of true magic, and was essentially evil in its aims and practices. It was based almost entirely on the desecration of Holy things, and only differed from sorcery in that it was practised by more educated and therefore more dangerous adepts. The Devil-Myth and worship of the king of evil, and both sexual and scatological practices played a great part in Black Magic proper, and necromancy naturally falls under this heading. Black magic is a direct consequence of the God-Satan opposition, and its ceremonial was derived to a great extent from this principle of opposition or inversion, examples of which may be found in such practices as reading the mass backwards, and considering as sacred the foulest objects imagination could devise.

Having examined and analysed these various headings and obtained some idea of their true intent and meaning, we shall then give an outline of the modern science of metapsychics.

The relation between past and present will then, I hope, be clearly established, and the great mass of legends and lore connected with the past, magicians, sorcerers, and witches, ghosts and hauntings, vampires and ghouls, will hold no terrors or mysteries any longer. If I can achieve this object and reduce the awe-inspiring lore of the past to its proper relative importance, I shall feel that I have accomplished something, that I have swept away the dark and loathsome obstacle that lies in the way of a clear understanding of those laws which have surrounded our lives with phenomena as yet unexplained, but which are now at least understood.

CHAPTER II

RELIGIOUS SYMBOLISM AND
THE DAWN OF RELIGION

'Religions ate the unconscious depositories of the wisdom of primitive civilisations.'

I HAVE said something concerning the growth and origin of religion in the preceding chapter and attempted to show the bearing of religion, and therefore of symbolism, on the subject of these essays. Both magic proper as I have defined it and witchcraft, both black magic and the sabbat, have their origin in some form or other of religious belief.

It is a matter of considerable difficulty to state what the earliest form of worship or religious system may have been; in fact we cannot even tell what the earliest forms of human thought may have been. It is not necessary for our purpose to go back so far; we are primarily concerned with those primitive doctrines on which the later complex religious structure was built and from which arose a multiplicity of cults and creeds, of philosophical and religious systems.

The fundamental principles from which religion originated, although they are few in number, are not necessarily the same for all races. Some possessed purely material religions for a considerable time, while others introduced into their systems of worship a pure philosophical conception at an early date.

The genesis of any religious system can be briefly summarised as follows: –

Two material factors, natural demonology and ancestral worship, lead gradually to an abstract threefold philosophy, the conception of an active principle, the necessary balancing conception of a passive principle, and equally necessary conception of a bond between the two. This idea, the conception of a soul, a body, and a bond between body and soul may be taken as the first important step towards the elaboration of a true religious system.

The natural demonology that pre-exists and coexists easily finds its place when the new doctrine appears. This new idea or principle, too abstract for general distribution, is quickly reduced to the level of common understanding by being endowed with personality, just as, in the same way, natural demonology arose from the creation of gods – spirits in essence – but concrete individuals to represent ideas and natural phenomena.

In this way we get triformed deities or three-headed gods, or groups of three powers, such as the Osiris-Amon-Ptah of Egypt, or again, family relations of three gods or powers. Sometimes the philosopher who first propounded the doctrine is worshipped as a god, as was the case with Buddha, but in all cases the demons and spirits of the primitive polytheistic creeds persist in the form of demi-gods, minor gods, or saints and heroes. They are given consorts, and legend follows upon legend as they materialise, until they become real tangible individuals, with a history and a definite existence.

From this creed. Ego – Non Ego – Affinity of the Ego for the Non Ego, or Essence of things – Matter of things – Bond, or Soul – Body – Intellect, it is but a step to Man – Woman – Love.

Thus do we get the first great ramification of religious systems. Phallic worship, which has left such a deep imprint on the history of the world.

Symbolism, the importance of which cannot be too strongly stressed, is the natural result of this tendency to express abstract ideas in concrete form, and the structure of any religious system is due to this materialisation of an abstract conception generally by means of personification, further elaborated by symbolical legend and attempts to fit into a single scheme the complex potentialities of man and nature.

Now the very essence of the ternary creed is the law of balance, and this gave rise, but at a considerably later period, to another great religious fallacy which left perhaps an even deeper imprint on the world, the Devil-Myth.

We are now in a position to justify the remarks on terminology made in the introductory chapter. Too many writers have grouped indiscriminately under such headings as 'Magic', 'Sorcery' or 'Witchcraft' a number of manifestations which have neither the same origin nor the same form. In order to get a clear insight into the apparently complex structure of occult science, it is necessary to discriminate very carefully between these various classes of belief.

Magic proper arose from the original Trinity-Unity doctrine. Black Magic arose from the God-Devil opposition. Sorcery was merely a reminiscence of cruder primitive cults coupled with a knowledge of drugs and poisons.

The evolution of early religions, divested of their apparent complications, schisms, and ramifications, can therefore be reduced to a primitive polytheism, and an early trinitarian conception, a hybrid combination of which produced the sexual cult, and the Devil-Myth.

Religions, cults, and creeds of the most varied nature can be traced back to these four fundamental principles.

Although it is true that the priests alone understood its significance, it may appear strange at first sight that such an abstract doctrine should have been conceived during the very early stages of human thought; there is every reason to suppose, however, and much evidence to support the fact, that one of man's first conscious realisations was the existence of a 'soul' or inner immaterial being or entity.

The most primitive tribes believe in the soul. The most primitive minds had within them the necessary material for a trinity, they were aware of the soul's existence, they possessed a body, they were capable of intelligent thought and therefore realised that there was a bond between the two – intelligence.

We find evidence of the belief in a 'soul' in a continuation of life in a new world, in the innumerable and elaborate burial rites of tribes and nations at all times and in all parts of the world. Moreover, dreaming must soon have enlightened primitive man in this respect, and this first idea of a soul, of something besides and beyond the material, helped him to conceive and believe in those gods and demons that were to him as the souls behind the sun, the heavens, the storms, the earth. Indeed, the spiritual creed may well have been conceived before primitive man ever realised the fact that the function of sex was to create life. We know that there are tribes in Australia to this day who are unaware of the relation between sexual connection and childbirth, whereas these same natives not only believe in the soul, but also in quite an elaborate system of metempsychosis, and in guardian angels and familiar spirits similar to the 'fravashi' of the Persians.

Ferdinand von Reitzenstein thinks that there was a time when the connection between cohabitation and pregnancy was unknown to all mankind, and many examples show that traces of such a state are to be found in the customs of many people. One of the origins of the doctrine of metempsychosis may have been this very difficulty, and ancestral worship can possibly be traced to the same source, although, in another form, it is a necessary adjunct to the doctrine of metempsychosis and reincarnation, as will be shown in another chapter.

Originally, man could not conclude from the mere appearance of a pregnant woman that the cohabitation that had occurred months ago was the cause of her condition. Besides, by far the greater number of cohabitations do not lead to pregnancy. Even among comparatively enlightened races this led to the assumption that some additional supernatural process is necessary for fertilisation. Among the Australians, the least developed race of men, the necessity of cohabitation for pregnancy is totally unknown. Baldwin Spencer and Frank J. Gillen have shown (1899, p. 123; 1904, pp. 145, 606) that among the natives of Central Australia there exists a general belief that children penetrate into the woman as minute spirits. These spirits are said to come from persons that have lived once before and are reborn in this manner.

In order to show how tribes ignorant of so simple a physical fact as the act of generation can yet elaborate complex mystic systems similar to the teachings of the most advanced schools of later times, we will carry the subject a little further. (Fig. 1.)

Among the Arunta, who live in the district between Charlotte Waters and the McDoimel Mountains, there exists a tradition that in bygone times, was called 'alcheringa', the male and female ancestors of the tribe carried about with them spirit children which they put down in certain places. These spirit children, like the spirits of the tribal ancestors themselves, enter into the women and are borne by them. The Arunta believe that at the death of a person his spirit returns to a special tree or rock, which is called ' nandcha' and out of which it came. It remains there until it thinks fit once more to enter a woman and thus go among the living. All these spirits are called 'iruntarinia', but before the rebirth of an iruntarinia there arises another spirit from the nandcha which is the double of the iruntarinia and is called 'arunburinga'. This arunburinga never becomes embodied but remains in spirit form and accompanies its human representative whenever inclined and, as a rule, remains invisible. Only specially gifted people or witch doctors can see them. Among other Australian tribes who believe in rebirth no belief in spirits like the arunburinga has been traced. (Fehlinger, *Sexual Life of Primitive People*, London, 1921. Compare *Totemkult und Seelenglauben bei Afrikanishen Volkem. Zeitschrift fur Ethnologie, Jahrgang* 50, p. 89.)

Here, then, is a clear case of reincarnation, and its origin would certainly seem to be ignorance of the process

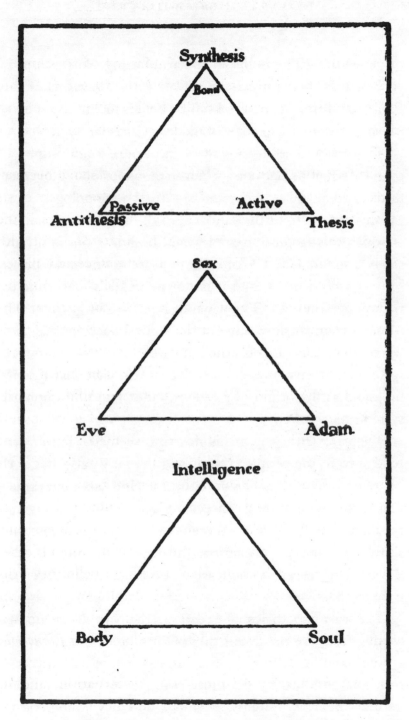

FIG. 1. FUNDAMENTAL TRIANGLE SYMBOLS

of generation. The belief in the arunburinga, moreover, is very curious, being precisely similar to the Fravashis of the Parsees and almost universal similar beliefs in familiar spirits, of which the guardian angel of modern Christianity is a form.

There would seem to exist, then, a purely philosophical origin of religions, one born of human thought alone, altogether distinct from, and as important as, natural demonology.

Any attempt to fix the date or even the approximate period at which this factor appeared would be futile; one can only say it is so old as to be common to all religions and cults in some form or other, and it is not necessarily posterior to natural demonology. The dawn of human thought is as yet too uncertain to allow any but the wildest speculations, and we are not so much concerned in dates, or in the manner in which this primary system arose, as in the fact that it is to be found at the origin of religions, cults, and philosophical systems the world over.

The care with which this doctrine seems to have been hidden from the people even during the very early stages is not due to anything inherent to the doctrine itself, but rather to its very simplicity and consequent lack of appeal to any but the higher intellects. It was therefore necessary to enclose this simple doctrine in a mysterious shrine, and surround it with the awe and respect without which no religion can have any hold on the masses.

The various stories of creation, the various religious writings that are the foundation of all religious systems, the symbols and legends of the past are based solely on this one principle enriched by the more complex astronomical and natural theurgic systems, enlarged and developed, often distorted and misunderstood, by priests and teachers, by tradition and inter-reaction. The flowery Eastern languages lent their naturally poetical expressions in order that the abstract creed, or rather the gods that had already replaced it, should be exalted and described in parable and legend. Into these legends were woven the countless threads of natural demonology, and half-forgotten tales of bygone civilisations and events were combined for the production of such beautiful creations as the Vedas of India.

Many investigators attempting to trace back religious systems to their origin have let themselves be lured into side alleys such as sex-worship or the Good and Evil opposition; yet neither of these is the true keystone of religious structures nor the ultimate meaning of religious symbolism. Both of these highly important phases of religious thought became so predominant as to blot out entirely the original doctrine from which they sprang till, indeed, no connection could be found between them.

Though it is true that sex-worship found its popularity and a favourable field for development though its intimate connection with natural demonology as distinct from any philosophical system, yet the fact that the Man-Woman-Generative Function combination was an exact counterpart or living symbol of the doctrine gave it further impetus and an obvious *raison d'etre*. It was a blind, a political or tribal necessity, and a concrete human religion such as would appeal to primitive civilisations when the more subtle and purely spiritual doctrines could never be understood, or if by chance some glimmer of their meaning was perceived it would be taken as just that sex-worship which was everywhere prevalent at the time.

That the mysteries of Eleusis were sexual in form there can be little doubt, although the same cannot be said for certain similar Egyptian mysteries, but whether the initiates of these rites were aware of their true meaning, since the phallic form was merely a veil, or whether the priests and originators alone grasped the symbolical significance of these ceremonies, is a question to which there seems to be no answer at present.

Abstract notions of divinity were of little avail to primitive people whose immediate tendency was to endow any idea or phenomenon with personality, and that personality with qualities and defects, with moods and habits. Many of the more fearful or horrible deities to be found principally in India, such as Kali and the existence of sects similar in nature to the Thugs, can be explained by this worship, not of a deity in the true sense of the word, but of an entity representing one particular mood of the deity. We can express this crudely by saying that committing murder from religious motives means propitiating God when He is in an angry or murderous mood. That these mood worshippers finally came to regard their god as a separate entity is only natural, and the process is similar to the worship of a multiplicity of Buddhas that arose from statues of the one Buddha in which he was pictured at different stages of his life, or with different attributes.

Let us now return to the examination of the original creed and clearly understand its meaning, since its various interpretations and S5rmbolical representations will give us the key to much that is obscure.

The Unity is represented by three terms which form the basis of all theurgic systems and which designate the same principles under a multitude of different forms and names.

The first of these terms represents Absolute Activity, and finds expression in various systems as Osiris, Brahma, Jupiter, God the Father, etc.

The second term represents Absolute Passivity, or nature, and finds expression in various systems as Isis, Vishnu, Juno, or God the Son, God-made Man.

The third term is the union, bond, or relation that must exist between the two first, and was expressed as Horns, Siva, Vulcan, or the Holy Ghost.

Expressing this idea in a still simpler and more abstract form, we may say that it is impossible to conceive the existence of an active principle or spirit, or immaterial element, of an Ego, except through its opposition to a non-Ego, or material, or passive element, and that this necessary opposition gives rise to another factor, which is the affinity or bond existing between the two.

The Trinity is the synthetic and absolute formula towards which all primitive sciences converged, and has been transmitted to us by all the religions in the world. Such is the simple creed which is the very foundation of all religious systems, teachings, sacred books, symbols, and initiations. It is stated above in its most abstract and general form, and, directly applied in this form, it constitutes the Great Arcana of Magic and religious initiations, the divinity of the living universe as represented by the universal or, better, comprehensive soul, the necessary corresponding material term, or life, and the bond between the souls of men as a whole and life as a whole, or the idea of God the Universe, which has sometimes been incorrectly expressed as the 'Divinity of Man.'

This principle may be expressed diagrammatically as shown in the Synthesis-Antithesis-Thesis triangle which plays so great a part in symbolism all over the world.

From this more general theogony the ancient philosophers passed on to a less general but more concrete androgony as expressed by the Body-Soul-Intelligence triangle in one form, and by the Adam-Eve-Sex triangle or Man-Woman-Generative Function triangle in another. As we shall see further on, a triangular cosmogony was evolved on exactly the same principles.

Man, regarded synthetically, is composed of an active animated body. If we think of man as a body only, without reference to its animation, or to its faculty of acting, its reality immediately disappears, it is no longer a man. If in the same way we wish to imagine by itself the principle which animates this body, which makes it live, the reality again disappears. It is impossible for us to separate the life from the idea of the body, to conceive what this thing may be which is called the human life, if we wish to see in it a kind of metaphysical being.

The difficulty increases considerably if it be a question of the principle which causes the body to act, of the soul. Analysis here, as elsewhere, can be brought into use, but we cannot possibly conceive what the soul can be like divested of form, that is to say of a principle that differs from itself. We picture to ourselves a small sphere, a winged head, in fact anything according to individual fancy, but never the soul considered individually.

On the other hand, the moment we say 'a Man' these three terms thus synthesised assume consistence and become the expression of the reality, a being formed of a body, a life and a will defines itself quite clearly.

Such was the primitive doctrine of universal balance, of action and reaction, and, needless to say, the innumerable examples of its actual truth and reality in everyday life expressed as a mechanical or physical law resulted in its being quickly considered as the synthetical expression of all science, wisdom, and religion.

The very great tendency which primitive civilisations show towards generalising and condensing, or expressing as a Synthetical symbol such knowledge as they acquired, must always be borne in mind, and it must also be remembered that, considering the small amount of scientific knowledge at their disposal, this tendency to express a general law for the apparently simple phenomena that came under their observation was a very natural one indeed. To the modern scientist the world is an extremely complex entity. He has long realised the enormous labour to be expended before man can begin to understand the mechanism of nature. But to the philosopher of old the world seemed a very simple thing, the more so since the greater number of phenomena were attributed to supernatural agencies. The extraordinary development of modern science and the greatly improved tools and methods now at the disposal of investigators have only shown us how vast and intricate the problem really is, or perhaps how apparently intricate, whereas the primitive thinker only saw nature in its magnificent outward simplicity. The outstanding facts for a philosopher of those times would be the law of balance and relationship we have just mentioned, and the four forms of matter: fire, air, water, and earth. This gives us a preliminary clue to the meaning of the earlier forms of symbolism, the square, or number four, and the triangle and trinity. There is a further explanation of the quaternary term as we shall see later. The greatest and most obvious example of this ternary-quaternary symbolism is given by the Pyramids, with their square bases and triangular faces, the only geometrical solid which would fulfil the necessary conditions, while the Sphinx again gives us a synthetical expression for the four forms .of matter, the wings for air, the body of a bull for the earth, a woman's breasts for the passive principle or water, and a lion's claws for fire. The Sphinx, however, is a complex symbol, like so many of the old symbols, and was intended to convey not one but a number of different meanings. It can be taken as a symbol of man arising from the animal form, and already aspiring to the spiritual, while it is also a trigram, the symbol of mind, body, and soul. The Sphinx was, moreover, the symbol of Egyptian initiation, and possibly the actual sanctuary where initiation took place. The initiatic tests consisted of rites during which the neophyte was required to demonstrate his control over fire, water, earth, and air. The human head of the Sphinx meant: 'First acquire that knowledge which points out the goal and lights the way to it.' The bull's thighs, image of the rough persevering labour of the agriculturist, meant:

'Be strong and patient.' The lion's claws meant:

'Thou must brave all and defend thyself.' The eagle's wings meant: 'Thou must will to raise thyself towards the transcendent regions which thy soul already approaches.'

I have stated that there was another reason for the importance of the number four in religious symbolism, and in order to understand its nature clearly we must examine the esoteric theory of numbers as studied by ancient philosophers. It should be remembered that these numerical systems were propounded at a much later date than the original triad and elementary tetrad, and only reached full development at the time of Pythagoras.

Such systems could obviously not be developed in very primitive times when men counted probably only up to ten, and for the full operation of these methods a digital system or partly digital notation is essential. Moreover, these systems flourished more especially among such nations as used a common notation for their letters and numerals, as in the Hebrew language, for instance.

But the more important facts concerning the first ten numbers (others in digital systems being merely a repetition) could certainly have been deduced by the most primitive tribes counting with the help of their fingers from one to ten. In connection with parity and imparity, definite and indefinite numbers, the old philosophers were deeply imbued with the union of numerical ideas with nature in its common acceptation, and also with nature's essences, or substrata of things.

The nature of good to them was definite, the nature of evil indefinite, and the more indefinite the nature of the evil the worse it was. There can be no doubt that the ancient Egyptians were fully aware of the mysteries connected with numbers.

The Monad, or one, was the principle and element of numbers, the father of numbers, the male principle, the intellect, the symbol of God and the sun. The Duad, or number two, was the universal mother, nature, the passive principle.

The Triad, or first odd number, was of very great importance, as has been already mentioned. It is impossible to study any system of worship without being struck by the peculiar persistence of the triple number in connection with divinity; three forms of habitation for the soul, triformed deities, three-headed gods, mysterious trinities, deities of three powers such as the Osiris-Amon-Ptah of the Egyptians, or family relationships of three powers. We have already explained the meaning of the triad, it is the synthesis of a positive principle, its corresponding negative reaction and the bond between the two. The triad also contains the three necessary dimensions for the definition of our three dimensional world, and this fact again gave it a greater importance in the numerical systems of old.

We must now consider what is known as theosophical addition and reduction. The whole numerical systems of such philosophers as Pythagoras, and of the initiations of ancient Egypt, are based on these operations.

Reduction consists in reducing all numbers formed of two or several figures to a number of a single figure, which is done by splitting the number into its constituent digits and adding these together. Should the number thus formed still contain more than one figure the operation is repeated till only one figure remains.

For example: –

$$10 = 1+0=1$$
$$11 = 1+1=2$$
$$12 = 1+2=3$$
$$126 = 1+2+6=9$$

$$2488 = 2+4+8+8=22=2+2=4$$

The second operation, or addition, consists in ascertaining the value of a number by adding together arithmetically all the figures from unity to itself inclusively.

For example: –

$$4 = 1+2+3+4=10$$
$$7 = 1+2+3+4+5+6+7= 28$$

Applying reduction to this last example, we get

$$28 = 2+8=10=1$$

These operations may appear to be entirely arbitrary, and so in fact they are. But by applying these two rules to numerals the old philosophers obtained some very curious results which by themselves perhaps would not have seemed to them so important, but which, when taken in conjunction with those primary principles we have already mentioned, gave them still further reason to believe in the truth and general application of their systems.

Reduction shows that all numbers are reducible to the nine first. Addition combined with reduction shows that the numbers 1, 4, 7, 10, 13, etc, can all be reduced to the monad or 1.

Thus: –

$$1 \qquad\qquad\qquad =1$$
$$4 = 1+2+3+4 = 10 = 1+0 = 1$$
$$7 = 1+2+3+4+5+6+7 = 28 = 2+8 = 10 = 1+0 = 1$$
$$10 = 1+0 = 1$$
$$13 = 1+3 = 4 = 1+2+3+4 = 10 = I+0 = I \text{ etc.}$$

In other words, these operations have shown us that every fourth number ultimately returns to the figure 1.

Thus: –

1	2	3		4	5	6	
4		=10=1		7		=28=10=1	
7	8	9		10	11	12	
10		=1		13		= 4 =10=1	

and so on.

The results are:

(1) That all the numbers in their evolution reproduce the first four.

(2) *That the last of these first four numbers represents unity in a different form.*

We may sum up the preceding statements by saying that the numbers may be reduced in final analysis to the series of the first four thus arranged: –

$$1 \quad 2 \quad 3$$
$$4$$

The reader will easily realise the immense importance of the results in view of what has already been said concerning the numbers 1, 2, 3, and 4. If we now express the philosophical meaning of these arithmetical operations it will be seen that we arrive at precisely the same conclusion as before, concerning the first three numbers, and we find a very important addition in the fourth, as we will now show.

Unity represents the creative principle, but unity alone cannot produce anything save by opposition to itself, hence duality, the passive principle. From the union of the unity and duality arises the third principle which unites the two opposites in a common neutrality, 1+2=3. Three is the neutral principle, and the bond between the active and passive principles. But these three reduce themselves into a fourth term, which merely represents a new form of the unity as an active principle. The fourth principle represents the transition necessary for the continuation of the progression or cycle, it represents the bond between one individual trinity and the next, the germ of a new active principle, in fact, the regenerative or productive principle.

The numerical system has in fact led us to the same conclusions which we deduced from the primitive abstract reasoning, and the tetrad has assumed a new importance.

It contains the active principle, the passive principle, the bond or neutral principle, the transitory productive germ, the Soul-Matter-Intelligence trinity, the Adam-Eve-Sex trinity, and the four elements that constitute our universe. The tetrad thus expresses in symbolical form those general laws with which the people were familiar, the law of balance, the four elementary forms of matter, life and death, soul and matter.

The idea of the cycle of life and of continuity must have come very naturally to early thinkers; the regular succession of day and night, of death and birth, of the seasons, were as many examples ever present to their minds. This idea of continuity plays a very important part in religious symbolism. It was usually represented by a circle or by a serpent biting its own tail, the emblem of eternity.

The tetrad was represented as a cross, and these two symbols are the earliest complete forms of synthetical theology and are common to all cults either separately or in a combined form (*crux ansata*).

All versions of Genesis contain at the very beginning a description of the Garden of Eden. The true translations and the older texts show a single tree before the Fall, but two trees after the Fall. The tree represents the universe, life and science of all things as one entity, and the dividing of the trees into the tree of life and the tree of science or knowledge, which occurs after the Fall, is a very significant fact. At the origin, however, we find but one tree, the emblem of the living universe, and from the foot of the tree there flow four rivers. This is the earliest symbol expressing those laws which we have mentioned and is, of course, the origin of the cross.

Attempts to convey the impression both of continuity and movement, or the eternal progression of life led to combinations of the circle and tetrad under various forms. The proportions of the cross and circle were themselves varied in order to give as many repetitions of the tetrad principle as possible, and these arrangements gave the particular proportions of the cross which is familiar to modern religion. Finally, as religious systems were elaborated and evolved, and astronomy was imported from Chaldea, these first basic ideas gradually developed and became more elaborate till we find the remarkable complex symbol illustrated, one of the most complete of its kind, an analysis of which will show us the meaning and origin of many obscure symbols. (Fig. 2.)

On examining this symbol we find that the idea of the universe has been developed and elaborated so as to show the twelve signs of the Zodiac, the five planets. Mars, Venus, Mercury, Saturn, and Jupiter, the Sun as the centre of the universe, and the Moon representing the female principle. The complete circle, taken in itself, also represents the Sun, and with the large Moon pictured is a second expression of the same idea considered as the heavens, an active principle in conjunction with, and in opposition to, the earth, represented by the cross and four elements. The whole figure is naturally a crux ansata, consisting of the tetrad and circle expressing once again the laws we have mentioned. The horns represent the transition term, or fourth term of the tetrad, or generative power of which we shall speak presently. Moreover, if we consider parts or portions of this symbol we immediately come upon the origin of those signs used by the ancients to denote the planets; this will be immediately apparent from the illustration.

Before proceeding any further, it will be necessary to retrace our steps for a moment and return to the original triad.

We have seen that this may be expressed in two different ways; in its most general sense, as an expression of the entire universe, or in a narrower sense as applied to man. Any system or symbol uniting these two expressions would then represent a perfect balanced formula containing the complete

FIG 2. VARIOUS EARLY SYMBOLS, ILLUSTRATING THEIR DEVELOPMENT

doctrine propounded by the old philosophers, or secret life. In other words, linking the two triangles we get what is known as Solomon's Seal or pentacle, the great emblem of all initiations. We have seen that according to the teachings to be found in the numerical systems the 4 is the germ of transition, the equivalent of 1, the perpetually active principle, and, if we consider 1 and 4 as two phases or forms of the same initial principle, we get a new figure or five-pointed star. If this be taken as representing the universe, it may be considered as bound together or balanced by either of the phases or forms of 1, i.e. Sex or Intelligence, passion or reason, and we now get some idea of how the worship of sex arose, where it did not pre-exist, and we see that it was substantiated by those very abstract systems the aim of which was its suppression. (Fig. 3.)

We can readily understand how sex became a simple explanation or interpretation of the old symbols, besides obviously being a popular form of worship and a necessity in times when an increase or otherwise in the number of its inhabitants meant the rise or downfall of a country.

We can understand, if we examine the planetary sign of Venus, how it is that so many writers have considered the crux ansata as a purely Phallic symbol; three attributes for the male, and the ring for the female.

It is therefore correct to state that the crux ansata was a Phallic symbol in this form, in those countries and at those periods in which Phallic worship prevailed; but the crux ansata was then only a part or portion of an older, more universal symbol, the true synthesis and origin of which we have shown, and a part that was devoted precisely to the cult of Venus.

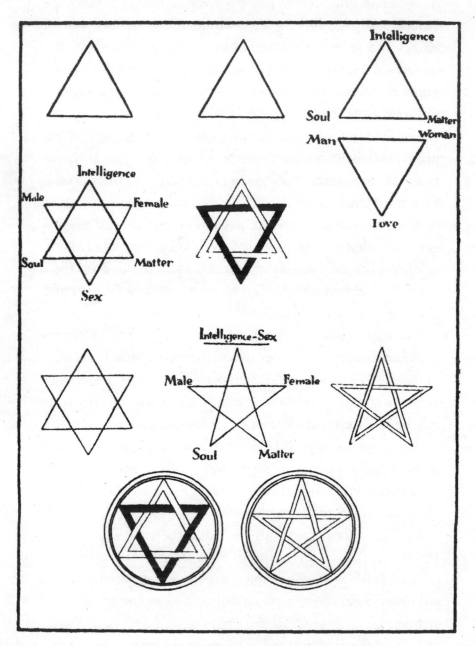

FIG 3. GENESIS OF PENTAGRAMS AND HEXAGRAMS

The same principles applied to other seemingly mysterious symbols will give us the inner meaning quite easily, and as an example let us consider the Hebrew name of God, yod-he-vau-he, of which so many fanciful explanations have been given at different times. The name is a complete tetragram or tetrad, and can be analysed as follows.

The YOD is the active principle or Ego, not the sex merely, nor the intelligence alone, but a continuous transitory cycle. The assertion of the Ego entails the realisation of the reaction of the Ego upon itself from which the conception of its existence will be drawn by a kind of division of the unity. The yod is here taken in its most complete form as 10, and its division gives 5, and the corresponding Hebrew letter he.

$$HE \quad YOD \quad 5 \quad 10$$

The HE represents the passive in relation to the yod which symbolises the active, the non-Ego in relation to the Ego, the woman in relation to man, substance to essence, life to soul. As we have seen, the opposition of the Ego to the non-Ego gives rise immediately to another factor, which is the affinity or bond existing between the Ego and the non-Ego.

Now the VAU, sixth letter, is produced by

$$YOD \quad HE=VAU$$
$$10+5=15=6$$

and thus we get the three first letters of the name

$$VAU \quad HE \quad YOD$$

6   5   10

The 6 is the link or analogy uniting two antagonisms in the whole of nature and completes the trinity.

Direct confirmation of this interpretation can be obtained by considering those Sephiroths of the Kabala that correspond to the numbers of the sacred name, 10 or I, 5, and 6.

The first and tenth Sephiroths are Wisdom, the male intelligence, the all-glorious presence. The fifth Sephiroth is the feminine potency, and the sixth is the uniting potency.

The last he represents the passage from one world to another, the transition; it may be compared to a grain of wheat relative to the ear; the ear, the trinity manifest, YOD-HE-VAU, exerts all its activity in the production of a grain of wheat or second HE, but this grain of wheat is only the transition between the ear that gave it birth and the ear to which it will itself give birth in the following generation, it is the transition between one generation and the other which it contains in germ. It is a repetition of the feminine term, in this particular tetragram as representing the pregnant female principle bearing the germ of a future generation, the new yod. It is in reality composed of the female 2 in conjunction with the germ of the new triad or 3. The continual transition or metamorphosis of the fourth term into the first gave rise to sex worship.

The triad or earliest synthetical symbol was not always expressed as a triangle, it was often expressed in the form of a simple architectural design of which the two pillars of the Temple of Solomon, Jakim and Boaz, with their cross-stone, are the best known example. One of the pillars expresses the active principle, the second the passive principle, and the cross-stone the bond. The whole of Solomon's Temple was, of course, entirely impossible as regards construction and was a parable or symbol, very complex in form and elaborate in detail, which contained the necessary laws and doctrines for setting up an ideal system of worship and universal government. The whole legend was woven around Hiram, and the loss of the cross-stone on which Freemasonry is based, the object of Freemasonry, 'to rebuild the Temple of Solomon' in the figurative sense (hence the name 'mason') is a remarkable instance of this symbolism, the meaning of which may be stated as being the loss of the bond or affinity between God and Man, the misinterpretation of the original creed, and the formation of schools of initiation who claim to preserve the true doctrine, as we shall see in a later chapter.

Many attempts have been made to explain the dolmens, but if an explanation is needed at all the most likely is to consider them as early forms of expression of the triad. Much has been made of these stone monuments of early civilisation, many more meanings have been drawn from them than they probably ever possessed.

What could be more natural for primitive man wishing to leave a permanent record of some important event, or mark the grave of some brave leader, than to erect a large stone, or two, or perhaps several. He may have been quite innocent of any further meaning, and if by chance he placed a third stone across the top of the two upright ones, is this not after all the simplest form and very dawn of architectures' And if after having built an arch he proceeded to build more contiguous arches till he had completed a vast circle, it is not at all obvious that it should be necessary to find some esoteric meaning to these activities which seem to explain themselves. It is very possible that stone pillars were used afterwards, or even erected in some cases for Phallic worship, and that the early architectural efforts of mankind were later used as places of worship for the very reason that the fundamental symbols were here already expressed; but the mere erection of large stones is a self-explanatory action and needs no further construing. The immense importance, interest, and universal character of symbolism cannot be too strongly stressed, but one can go to extremes and see symbols of the past where no such record was intended. The essential simplicity of the primitive symbols is for this reason a pitfall for the unwary.

Before we leave the subject a few words should be said about two very important and much-discussed symbols, namely, the winged sphere and the Swashtika.

The winged globe or sphere expressed the essence of all things, or God the Father. The serpent stood for the flesh, matter, and the wings stood for the spirit, or intelligence, or bond. The symbol is only complete inasmuch as it bears a snake under the sphere; it is one of the oldest triads and is very common in Egyptian symbolism. (Fig. 4.)

The Swashtika, one of the most discussed symbols in the world, is yet one of the most simple and easiest to explain. We find it both three-legged and four-legged; it is a trigram in the first case, a tetragram in the second. The legs and feet, when pictured, and the bending over of the cross arm extremities when the figure is diagrammatic, are merely added to indicate motion continuity, the cycle of life. It is merely a simpler

FIG 4. VARIOUS SYMBOLS BASED ON THE ORIGINAL TRIAD AND THE
CIRCLE OF CONTINUITY

form of synthetical symbol than the crux ansata in which the circle indicating the cycle of life has been replaced by the very effective method of giving the whole cross an indication of continuous movement or unidirectional rotary motion. The Swashtika considered in this light is certainly the clearest, most compact, and neatest of the symbols of the past, and if we picture it made up of curved lines, as it is often found, we have a figure consisting only of two intersecting curved lines, but which contains within itself the complete synthetical creed and doctrine that is the foundation of all religious and philosophical systems the world over. The inversion of the rotational movement as occasionally found is of particular interest and may be compared with the inverted pentagram as used in Black Magic. (Fig. 5.)

We have seen that apart from natural demonology there lies at the root and foundation of all religious systems a philosophical creed, everywhere the same, either pre-existing or elaborated at a later period. We have seen that this creed gives us a simple key to all the mysterious trinities that are to be found in religions and that it can be expressed as:

Ego-Non Ego-Affinity of one for the other.

We have also seen that this creed can be taken as expressing more generally the universe as a whole, and more particularly, man and life. We have seen that philosophers reasoning in a purely abstract fashion along these lines, and philosophers such as Pythagoras and the Egyptian initiates, reasoning by means of numerical operations, came to identically the same conclusions, and as a result the original creed was

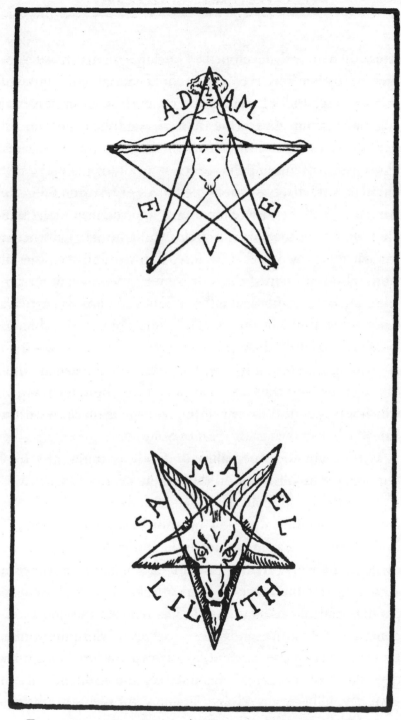

FIG 5. THE PENTAGRAM OF APPOLONIUS AND THE INVERTED
PENTAGRAM OF BLACK MAGIC

strengthened and developed. The laws of nature such as they were then observed and studied merely corroborated the doctrine, and it assumed the proportions of a universal dogmatic axiom. As Hermes puts it, 'Quod est inferius est sicut quod est superius' (*Tabula Smaragdina*). Life and the transmission of life, and the reduction of all figures to the first tetrad or tetractix, brought in the fourth or transition term in the tetrad, and the idea of continuity and rotation or cycle of life brought out the idea of a circle, while the original triad or triangle was now expressed as a cross, the four extremities of which also represented the four elementary forms of matter. The universal symbol thus became a crux ansata in some cases, a Swashtika in others. The same object was achieved by linking together the two triangles each of which was a triad containing one the universal, the other the particular form of the creed, and thus a symbol was formed the meaning of which was identical to that of the *crux ansata* and Swashtika and which is known as the Seal of Solomon.

It is impossible to realise in modern times just how important symbolism was to the ancient civilisations.

We find it difficult to understand how universal was the use of symbols and how prominent a part they played in literature, in art, in architecture, and in life in a number of different ways. At the present day man has amassed a very considerable stock of scientific knowledge based on patient gradual observation. He has realised the enormous complexity of nature, and set to work unravelling its secrets by methods of patient scientific analysis. But in those early days, far from realising the complexity of nature and natural laws, devoid of means of observing any but the most obvious phenomena, man looked on the universe and found it simple. He was struck by a certain number of apparently universal laws and facts, the four elements, the continuous cycle of life as shown by day and night, the movements of the stars and planets, life and death, or rather death and birth, that perpetual renewal or transition which is expressed in the tetrad, and he proceeded synthetically. The laws of nature, of life, of soul and matter were simple, he understood them, and he proceeded to express them, to condense them into simple diagrams, synthetical signs representing the Science-Wisdom of his age, the alpha and omega of all things. These symbolical expressions, which were in his eyes a complete image of the universe, were the highest and purest expression of human thought, the greatest achievement of which he was capable. We can no longer wonder, then, at the number of these symbols all identical in meaning and often very different in form; we cannot wonder that in the early efforts of architectural art some form of these symbols should be used as a theme, the proportions of chambers chosen in accordance with certain numerical laws governed again by these same symbols, great monuments set up proclaiming to an unseeing world what they considered to be the universal truth.

*   *   *

As an illustration of the close alliance of the triangle symbolism with architecture and of the way in which this old tradition has been handed down through generations so that we find it in buildings of the Gothic period, I can do no better than quote an article by Arthur Bowes, A.M.INST.C.E., taken from *Discovery*, January 1922, and the correspondence exchanged in that journal between the author and F. C.

Mears, of the College of Art, Edinburgh. Mr. Bowes's second letter is particularly suggestive.

'In architecture, as distinct from building construction, the relative proportions of the different parts of a building are an essential factor if it is to embody conceptions of beauty or any suggestions by the use of symbols. Measurement and the adoption of units of measurement thus become necessities in the primeval stages of art. In the July issue of Discovery I showed how the Hexalpa or six-pointed star, the Pythagorean or 3, 4, 5 triangle, and other simple geometrical figures were largely used in the early stages as unitary measures and how also these fundamental figures can still be traced in the design of structures where their presence has been hitherto unsuspected. I offer some further examples here in the hope of inducing more detailed investigations into a subject both wide in extent and historically interesting.

'The Hexalpa, or double triangle, or six-pointed star, is probably the most ancient of such unitary figures on account of the ease with which it could be constructed.

'It is based on the aggregation of equilateral triangles and would be formed in primitive times by the use of three measuring rods of equal length placed end to end. Strings or cords might have been used as we know that they were used very early in Egyptian civilisation, but the measuring rod is one of the most venerable appliances. It still exists among us, if only in name, as the ' rod, pole or perch ' of land measure. In setting out the Hexalpa on the site of a budding the process would be something like the following: The centre point would be first determined upon and the triangle ABC formed by placing the rods end to end as in the figure. The rod AC being left in position, AB and BC would be transferred to new positions in order to form triangle ACD, and so on until the whole figure was completed. The accuracy would be checked by the closing in on the first and last triangles and also by the prolongation of the lines to the outside points or 'landmarks' indicated by 1, 2, 3, 4, 5, 6. The use of the Hexalpa has been so largely dealt with in architectural literature that it will be sufficient here to call attention to some examples not referred to by other authors. In Lincoln Cathedral the vertical section of the south transept is based on three hexagons such as form the central part of the Hexalpa. The ground plan of Coningsburgh Castle is obviously a hexagon. In the Rhine valley the churches of Treves, Speyer, and Freiberg have three plans based on either one or two hexagons. It is especially interesting to find by the examination of the plans of Sir E. A. Wallis Budge's Handbook of the Nile that the temples of Karnac, Medinet Habu, and Denderah reveal the same method of planning. The revival of classic architecture gave birth to a multitude of arbitrary rules derived from the study of the first buildings of Greece and Rome, in the hope of emulating their beauty or proportion. Some of these rules, even when divorced from classic design, remained in use until the Victorian age. Thus it was held that beauty of design in any rectangle, such as a window opening, or panel, was ensured when the width and length equalled respectively the side and the diagonal of a square, that is to say 1 to 1.414. For simplicity of approximation 7 to 10 was used.

'The construction of a right angle by means of a triangle whose sides were in the ratio 3:4:5 was a process familiar to the ' rope-stretcher ' or surveyor of Egypt, China, and India in the earliest stages, and the influence exercised by this figure on the design of buildings was considerable.'

Before we quote any further from this article we must see what other significance the 3:4:5 triangle has besides being a triangle giving a right angle by the simple process of laying down its three sides which are all simple whole numbers. That it has another significance is obvious since it would have been just as easy to lay out an equilateral triangle and construct a right angle by division of the base into two equal parts. We have seen that the Pyramids with their square bases and triangular faces were expressions of the triad and tetrad combined. If then in such a Pyramid the faces form equilateral triangles, the triangle containing the height and slope will be almost exactly a 3:4:5 triangle. We shall see confirmation of this point in the remainder of the article, the quotation of which we will now resume. (Fig. 6.)

'Some further examples of its use are now offered, but to show in detail the various methods in which it was applied would necessitate more space. The references then are intended chiefly as indicating where confirmation of the statements of its use may be found. If the plans of York Minster be examined it will be seen that three diamonds each formed of four 3:4:5 triangles with their four right angles in juxtaposition, will fill the width and length of the nave from the west end to the altar, and another half diamond will complete the length to the east of the building. In Beverly Minster, and possibly in Newark Church, the same figure determines the principal proportions. In the church at Bradford-on-Avon, built by St. Aldhelm in the eighth century, the dimensions of the chancel are also based on this same figure. A building which is permeated throughout by this root figure is Magdalen College, Oxford.

'The most interesting of all discoveries, and one which lifts the theory into the domain of public interest, is that which clearly establishes its relation to the Pyramids of Egypt. It is generally supposed that if anything can give weight to a new idea no argument can surpass the calling in of the Pyramids as witnesses of the truth. Their confirmatory evidence is conclusive. Let me then describe the manner in which this venerable enigma of the builder's lore lurks unseen by the average eye in the unchanging lineaments of the Pyramids. For some years I tried unsuccessfully to find a relation between the slope of the Great Pyramid and any of the angles of the 3:4:5 triangle. Failing in that direction, I directed my attention to some of the others

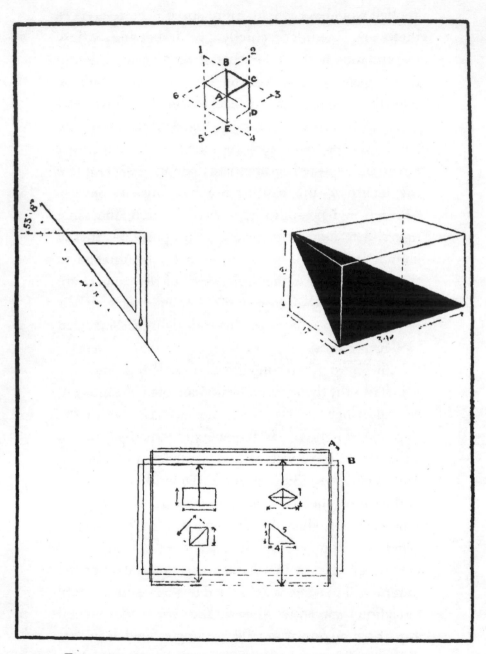

Fig 6. ARCHITECTURAL IMPORTANCE OF THE 3: 4: 5 TRIANGLE

out of the many Egyptian Pyramids and met with the following extraordinary result. In the Encyclopedia Britannica the slope of the second Pyramid, that of Kephron, and also that of the seventh, eighth, and ninth Pyramids, is given as 53 degrees 10. The discrepancy between this value and the angle of the 3: 4: 5 triangle, that is 53 degrees 8, is as a matter of material practice so small that there is little reason to doubt that in the building of these Pyramids the 3: 4: 5 triangle was used to regulate the slopes. (Also incidentally making the faces equilateral. – C. W. O.)

'Even in the Great Pyramid itself, although the slope of the side cannot be made to conform to this theory, there lies a cryptic revelation of the 3:4:5 triangle hidden in the dimensions of the King's Chamber, the very nucleus of the stone immensity. The dimensions of the King's Chamber are 34 by 17 feet, with a height of 19 feet. The floor is a simple oblong, twice as long as it is wide. The curious relation of width to height leads to the discovery that an imaginary 3:4:5 triangle will exactly fit into the chamber if the 4 side is assumed to lie along the foot of one of the side walls with the opposite angle of the triangle raised until the 5 side forms the solid diagonal of the chamber. The statement is not an airy creation of fancy. If the measurements on which the calculations are based are correct, and there is no reason to doubt their accuracy, then the result is a mathematical certainty. The work of setting up the dimensions in this chamber would have been carried out more easily by cords than rods. Three of the priestly architects would determine the intended height of the chamber by the simultaneous stretching of two cords. Once the height had been determined the polished red granite blocks forming the walls would have been built in, the roof slabs laid, and the superstructure completed. The treasure buried in the heart of the Great Pyramid was not a hoard of gold or jewels that could be ransacked. It was entirely immaterial, an idea, not a tangible thing, and so it came about that after forty centuries of turmoil and change it rested there, an unsolved mystery.'

'There can be no doubt that the proportions of primitive architecture were worked out on systematic lines and probably by the aid of such figures as those suggested in the above article. I have made many attempts to get results in this collection but have always been checked, firstly by the difficulty of obtaining exact data, and secondly by the ease with which apparent solutions may be found. There are many possible unitary figures, but even if we restrict ourselves to the four mentioned, very slight errors in the plan under investigation may lead us to wrong conclusions. This difficulty is illustrated by the accompanying diagram which gives the four figures superimposed. It will be clear that any rectangular cells whose corners lie between the points A and B will in a large number of cases approximate very closely to one of the unitary figures. When in addition we remember that the builders may have set out their work on the outside face, the centre, or the inside face, we realise that the chances of correspondence will be greatly increased since we have a choice of three slightly varying rectangles on which we may apply our unit figures.'

F. C. Mears

'I am glad to have the opportunity of seeing the remarks of Mr. Mears and wish to express my agreement with him in his plea for caution in accepting results which may possibly be due only to coincidence or incorrect data. The diagram of four rectangles derived from different units, drawn with their edges overlapping on all sides, minimises the real difference in size. It is not thus that one compares the sizes of envelopes or cards. Instead of trusting to the drawn figures it would be safer to use the calculated proportions. For the rectangles formed from the four unitary figures named the ratios are such as to make it easy to investigate the measured dimensions. Corroborative arguments, however, are desirable, and guidance in this direction will be found in matters which I have refrained from introducing. I refer to considerations derived from history, religion, tradition, mythology, and symbolism, in fact from the sense of general fitness of the result. For example, Mr. Mears points out that the height of the King's chamber is almost exactly half the diagonal of the plan. This is mathematically correct, but the relation does not suggest any meaning or any reason for its presence. Also, it is not known to occur elsewhere. The 3:4:5 triangle on the other hand was intimately bound up with Egyptian art and thought.

In religion its three sides were associated with Isis, Osiris, and Horns. It was known to their land surveyors and architects from time immemorial, and in all likelihood they were acquainted with certain recondite uses of the triangle which, although they have been made public in the last few years, may still be said to be almost unknown to our age. One of the angles derived from it stands openly displayed in the slopes of neighbouring pyramids. The 3:4:5 triangle seems a particularly fitting symbol to be embodied in the King's chamber, and until a better solution presents itself I think we may leave it to occupy the position it now fills so adequately and unobtrusively.'

The above quotation is a direct confirmation of the remarks we have made concerning symbolism.

The ruins of Egypt are like the pages of a book written with temples, towns, obelisks, and Sphinxes for words and sentences. The very division of the land of Egypt was symbolical, the names of the provinces correspond to sacred numerical laws. The kingdom of Sesostris was divided into three parts: Upper Egypt representing the essence of all things. Lower Egypt representing matter, and Middle Egypt the land of Science and the higher initiations. Each of these three divisions was subdivided again into ten provinces each of which was under the protection of a god. These gods, thirty in number, and grouped three by three, were the symbolical expression of the triad within the decad: 1, 2, 3, 4. 4, 5, 6, 7. 7, 8, 9, 10. In other words, the triple meaning of the universal triad or tetrad, in its natural sense, in its philosophical sense, in its religious sense. The geographical division of the kingdom of Sesostris was in itself a symbol, a pentacle, an expression of the same principle which is to be found in the Pyramids or Sphinxes.

Before closing this chapter on symbolism it is necessary to examine briefly the Tarot, or divining cards.

Much doubt has been expressed concerning the antiquity or otherwise of the Taro cards, handed down by the gypsies from generation to generation. Such writers as Papus, William Postel, Count de Gebelin, Etteila, Eliphas Levi, J. A. Vaillant and others hold it to be the primitive book of ancient initiation or *Book of Thoth*. A discussion on the age or otherwise of the Taro would be out of place in these essays, and, moreover, it is not material to the subject. Waite states that there is no definite proof that the Taro cards existed before the fourteenth century, but this appears immaterial, for it is obvious even from a cursory examination of the Taro cards that they are concentrated symbolical expressions of pentacles as old as the world. Therefore, whether the Taro existed in the earlier days, or was elaborated at a later date, it was at any rate an extract and synthesis of the universal science, and, if not itself of great age, can only be the reproduction or expression of something that was.

The Taro pack is divided into two parts known respectively as the Minor and Major Arcanas.

The Minor Arcana consists of four suits: the Sceptres, the Swords, the Cups, and the Pentacles. Each suit consists of ten cards numbered from 1 to 10 and four court cards: the Knave, the Knight or Esquire, the Queen, and the King. The Major Arcana consists of twenty-two 'trump' cards whose denominations are: –

0 The Fool	11 Fortune
1 The Juggler	12 The Old Man
2 The High Priestess	13 The Hanged Man
3 The Empress	14 Death
4 The Emperor	15 The Devil
5 The Pope	16 Thunder
6 Love	17 The Star
7 The Chariot	18 The Moon
8 Temperance	19 The Sun
9 Justice	20 The Universe
10 Strength	21 The Angel

I shall not attempt to give the complicated theories which have been propounded concerning the meaning of each of the cards of the Major Arcana, and the methods of using the pack for the purpose of divination. I must refer the reader to the writers I have already mentioned, in whose works he will find some interesting facts connected with symbolism, and further confirmation of the statements made. I propose, however, briefly to show how the general plan of the pack was devised as a numerical expression of the tetrad which is the subject of this chapter.

If then in the Taro we consider the suits as a whole, they show us an application of what Pythagoras initiated in Egypt has called the tetractis, or sequence of the first four numbers which is the same as the sacred name YOD-HE-VAU-HE.

This same law is reproduced in each suit, it is present again in the four court cards of each suit, in the four series of numbers, and in the septenary division of the trumps forming the Major Arcana. The word Taro, moreover, is merely an anagram of the word rota, a significant fact in itself.

In one suit we get the combination: –

YOD			KING		SCEPTRES		
IIE	HE	QUEEN	KNAVE	CUPS	PENTACLES		
VAU			KNIGHT		SWORDS		
	1		4		7		
2		3	5	6	8		9
	4		7		10		

Representing yod we have: King, 1, 4, 7.
Representing First he we have: Queen, 2, 5, 8.
Representing vau we have: Knight, 3, 6, 9.
Representing Second he we have: Knave, 10.

In other words we have: –

Four Kings, four Aces, four Fours, and four Sevens, corresponding to the yod and suit of Sceptres, symbol of the Spiritual.

Four Queens, four Twos, four Fives, and four Eights, corresponding to the First he or suit of Cups, symbol of the Material.

Four Knights, four Threes, four Sixes, four Nines, corresponding to the VAU or suit of Swords, or symbol of Life.

And, finally:

Four Knaves and four Tens, corresponding to the Second he or suit of Pentacles, symbol of Transition or Generative Function.

Each series is complete in itself and contains a fourth or transition term to the next, thus if we consider four series of three numbers we are left with the Ten as a transition term, or the Knave in the case of the four court cards, or the suit of Pentacles in the case of the four suits. In other words, the Ten is the transition factor from suit to suit, the Knave from suit to court cards, and the Pentacles from Minor to Major Arcanas.

Applying the same principles to the twenty-one cards of the Major Arcana, the fool, or twenty-second card, being numbered 0, we note that the ternary combinations combine to give us three septenaries, and these, each having a figure common to the next, leave us with 19, 20, and 21, which, taken together, form the ternary of transition or Second he belonging to the three septenaries considered as a whole. This will be clear from the illustration. (Fig. 7.)

Such is the numerical basis on which the Taro is built up, and from numerical combinations and different interpretations of the twenty-two trumps and their combinations, a whole system of divination has been evolved for a description of which I must refer the reader elsewhere.

Immense importance was attached to numerical operations and combinations by the ancients, and the correspondence between words and the numbers obtained by substituting figures for the letters. These various numerical methods, combined with similar operations on astronomical observations, formed one of the most important branches of divination, other forms of which were the examination and interpretation of omens and dreams, a crude form derived from demonology, and trance or auto-hypnotic oracles, the

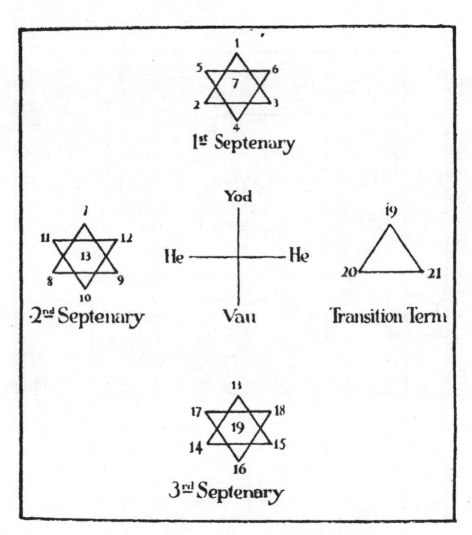

FIG 7. TARO CARDS, ARRANGEMENT OF TRUMPS

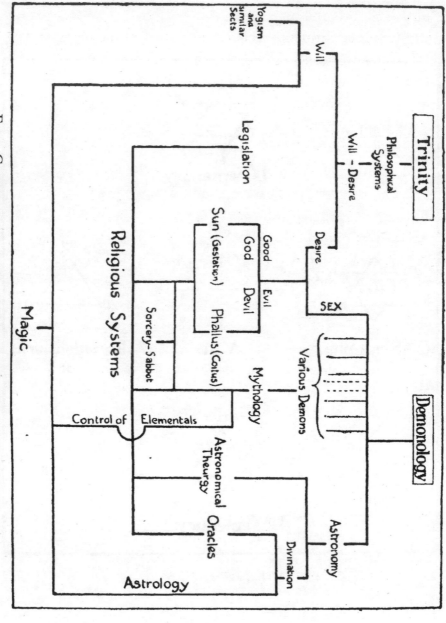

Fig 8. Chart illustrating development of religious systems

highest form of divination, a clear case of Cryptesthesis under autohypnotic conditions.

Further confirmation and substantiation of the numerical theories set out in this chapter, and of the existence at the origin of all symbolism of a trinitarian creed such as we have described and defined, will be found in the fact that the same ideas apply both to Sanscrit notations and to the Trigrams of FU HSI.

These numerical combinations, however, had a further import. They were used as a method for composing sentences, names, and complete word systems, which were then woven together by means of parables and symbolical legends to form books, the true esoteric meaning of which was thus hidden to all but those who held the key to the cipher.

One of the most remarkable examples of this is the Bible, or sacred book of the Hebrews, the Old Testament of Christianity, and it is more than probable that all sacred books were written on the same principle.

In the following chapter I have attempted to give some idea of how the Bible was written.

CHAPTER III

THE KABALA

'Une tradition des enfants de Seth emportée de Chaldée par Abraham, enseignée au sacerdoce Egyptien par Joseph, receuillie par Moise, et cachée sous des symboles dans la Bible, révélée par Jesus Christ à St. Jean et contenue dans l'Apocalypse, ceci est la Cabale.'

Eliphas Levi.

It is not my object in this chapter to enter into any discussion concerning the origin or age of the Bible, or into the origin or age of the Hebrew language.

Some writers trace it back to the fifteenth century B.C., others maintain that the whole book, and even the Hebrew language, was produced wholesale by the Romans in the early a.d. centuries as an attempt to create a universal world-binding religion with a view to strengthening a tottering empire.

In either case it remains an undisputed fact that the Bible contains the same symbolical parables and legends that are to be found in other and older sacred books throughout the religious systems of the world. If it should be true that the book was created by the Romans, then at any rate it was a copy or transcription of other sacred books.

Times beyond number men have devoted years of their lives in endeavouring to interpret the Bible one way or another, and any of these interpretations has undisputed evidence to support it, whether it be the Christian Science doctrine, the Catholic doctrine, or a purely sexual interpretation. The truth is that the very ambiguous nature of Biblical legends allows them to be twisted to fit any required meaning.

What all commentators seem to have ignored is that the Bible as it stands is absolutely incomplete, quite apart from the fact that it has in any case been so translated as entirely to alter the original sense. The Bible text as it stands in the original Hebrew is worthless by itself, except for the general trend of the symbolical stories it contains and which are but the outer form of all sacred books. Apart from its general symbolical form, the Bible text constitutes an elaborate cipher, an astonishing collection and combination of ciphers, in which no word, no sentence, no name can be taken literally.

The Hebrew initiates, foreseeing the fate which awaited this book and the false interpretations which would be given to it in the course of time, resorted to an oral law which was delivered to reliable men who were charged to transmit it to others in the secret of the Sanctuary. These in their turn transmitting it from age to age secured its preservation for the most distant posterity. This Oral Law which modern Jews still flatter themselves they possess is called the Kabala.

The Jewish Rabbis, then, discovered so much that was of interest behind the merely superficial value of numbers and of words and their interpretation that they developed a complete science of numerical conceptions apart from mathematics. This collection of ciphers, from which the Bible is written, is the Cabbala, or Qabalah, or Cabala, words variously misspelt from the Hebrew QBLH, meaning the received doctrine, or oral law, from the root QBL, meaning ' to receive.'

I am not proposing to give a complete description of the Kabala, my purpose is merely to point out as an illustration of the importance of numerical systems the impossibility of attempting any direct interpretation of Biblical texts.

The ciphers contained in the Kabala are divided into three parts, containing Gematria, Notaricon, and Temura. Gematria is a method depending on the fact that when the sum of the numbers of the letters composing a word is the same as the stun of the numbers of the letters composing another word, however different, an analogy is found between them and they are considered as having a necessary connection. In this way certain numbers were well known as meaning certain things, and not only words but whole sentences were treated in this manner.

Let us take a few examples.

Referring to Genesis xviii. 2 we find the words: –

'And lo, three men'
Vehenah shalishah
VHNH   SHLSHH
6   5   50   5   300   30   399   5=701

and

'These are Michael, Gabriel, Raphael.'
Alu Michael Gabriel ve Raphael
ALV   MIKAL   GBRIAL   VRPAL
I   30   6   40   10   20   I   30   3   2   200   10   I   30   6
200   80   I   39=701.

The three men were therefore Michael, Gabriel, and Raphael, and although those two sentences may be separated and even included in other sentences so that no connection appears, the inner meaning of perhaps several verses will be 'And lo, three men, these are Michael, Gabriel, and Raphael.'

Here again we are faced with a further difficulty; what is the true meaning of such a sentence, and of these names?

Even now it cannot be taken literally, for the following reason. Notaricon means the construction of a word from the initial or final letters of the several words of a sentence, or vice versa, the construction of a sentence of which each word in order begins or ends with one of the several letters composing a word or name. For example, referring to Deuteronomy xxx. 12 we find: –

'Who shall go up for us to Heaven.'
My Yeolah Lenu Hashemimha.
MY   YOLH   LNU   HSHMYMH.

The initials of the words give: mylh or mylah, meaning ' circumcision.'

The final letters of the words give: yhvh, meaning ' GOD,' suggesting that Jehovah pointed out the way to Heaven by Circumcision.

Again, the first six letters of the Book of Genesis are BRASHIT, translated ' In the beginning,' but more properly 'In Wisdom.' They are the initials of the words: –

BRASHIT RAH ALHIM SHYQBLV ISHRAL TVRII
Berasit rauah Elohim shyequebelu Israel torah.
In the beginning God saw that Israel would accept the Law.

Again, the famous Rabbinic name of power, agla, is formed from the initials of the words; –

ATH GBVR LOVLM ADNI
Atch gibur loulam Adonai
Thou art powerful throughout the ages. Lord.

We still have yet another difficulty to contend with, a most elaborate system of permutation ciphers collected under the name Temura.

Temura means permutation, sometimes the letters of a word are transposed according to certain rules, and with certain limitations sometimes each letter of a word is replaced by another according to a definite scheme, thus forming a new word.

For instance, the alphabet of 22 letters is halved and the two halves placed one over the other in reverse order; then A is changed to T, etc. It will be at once apparent that there are altogether 22 different ways in which this may be done. The various permutations are employed continually and indiscriminately. Moreover, other permutations are obtained by forming a square and subdividing it by 21 lines in each direction into 484 smaller squares, and then writing in each square a letter in order from right to left or above down, or the reverse, etc.

'Magic' squares and such combinations were also commonly used and various other less important forms of cipher.

The Greeks did not develop or use their letters as numbers for mental conceptions, yet in the Middle Ages we often find Greek letters used to transliterate Hebrew similars, so there was formed a bastard Greek Kabala on the Hebrew type.

In conclusion, I will give one or two typical examples of these numerical names that are of some interest.

Let us consider the names of JESUS and MARIA.

JESOUS	MARIA
10	40
8	1
200	100
70	10
400	1
200	
—	—
888	152

Now, taking the figure 152, let us set it out as a 'Magic ' square: –

$$
\begin{matrix}
1 & 5 & 2 \\
5 & 2 & 1 \\
2 & 1 & 5
\end{matrix}
$$

We immediately perceive that this square totals up all ways to 888.

It is therefore possible, though I am making no assertion, that the name of Jesus was obtained in this way, using the name of Mary as a starting point, or the reverse. Certainly the greater number of Biblical names were obtained by such methods, so that it is really of very little use to speculate as to their etymology or esoteric meaning.

Another curious example is that of the famous mystic word

'ABRACADABRA,' or rather ' abraxas.'

It will immediately be seen that on transferring it to numerals, and adding these together, the total number of days of the year is obtained, or one complete cycle of life.

ABRAXAS=1   2   100   1   60   1   200=365

I think I have said enough both to illustrate the predominant part played by numbers and corresponding letters, and to show that the Bible text is incomplete by itself. Unfortunately, the Kabala is merely a collection of elaborate ciphers which must have been used or applied according to some definite rule, but this rule or law governing their application which would give us the key to the true meaning of the Bible does not appear to be in the possession of mankind any longer.

This chapter has perhaps been somewhat of a digression, but it is justified as an illustration of the preceding one, and also because it shows that attempts at building up new religions based on various interpretations of Sacred Texts are foredoomed, and since the greater proportion of the world's religious systems and sects derive their doctrines precisely from this source, it may not come amiss.

CHAPTER IV

PHALLIC WORSHIP

'Turn Pater Omnipotens fecundis imbibis aether Conjugis ingremium laete descendit.'

Virgil, Geor. II.

The analysis of symbolism has led us to the consideration of two root principles of religious systems, Sex or Phallic worship and the Devil-Myth. The present chapter is concerned with the analysis of the first of these, the worship of the Phallus, the Priapic or Theophallic doctrine.

In order fully to understand the importance of Phallic worship we must examine closely its various forms and meanings and try to realise its true purport. That the original triad should have been taken literally in its material form will be readily understood, and we have seen that such was the case all over the world, but this alone is not sufficient to give us a satisfactory explanation of the way in which this doctrine spread amongst humanity. We have seen that this form of worship was popular inasmuch as it appealed to the people through its very nature and concrete material form, whereas the more abstract interpretation of the triad could never have taken any hold over mankind. We have also seen that a cult of this nature suited the purpose of the priests as a blind, and as a sure method of increasing the population.

But the important fact which must be grasped is that Phallic worship could never have taken the place it did had it not been the mere veil behind which glimpses could be caught of an inner, mysterious, carefully hidden doctrine. I am convinced that none but the most ignorant ever considered Phallic worship as anything in itself, nothing more than the worship of sex, and that the majority considered it only as the material, living prototype of a more abstract mystery, the true nature of which they may or may not have known. The ceremonial form, symbolism of Phallic worship, the legends connected with its origin and the way in which it arose all concur to substantiate this statement.

We have shown that according to the ancient doctrine the trinity or triad could be expressed either as Soul-Matter-Intelligence or as Man-Woman-Sex. The fourth term of the Tetrad was but a repetition of the first under a new form representing the transition or continuation principle, and the universe thus defined could be considered as balanced either by Intelligence or Sex. The combination of these meanings is to be found in the linked triangles and in the consequent pentagram, and it will be clear that predominance can be given to either the lower or upper triangle, to either the upright or inverted pentagram, that is to the abstract idea of Soul-Matter-Intelligence which must tend to exalt the moral and intellectual side of man, or to the Man-Woman-Sex idea, which must tend to exalt those material relations between male and female which create life.

But we must not suppose that adopting the second of these systems necessarily implies a negation of or an opposition to the first, though this may sometimes have been the case in certain forms of darker cults. On the contrary, we have every reason to believe that this second meaning became preponderant as an example, a prototype of the first, the importance of which was never lost sight of at the origin. There were many other reasons besides why Phallic worship should have spread so rapidly, but, in its widest sense, Phallic worship was the vast living symbol of a hidden creed, the symbolical, concrete, popular form of an abstract idea, and Sex in itself was not an object of worship so much as a convenient figurehead for what lay behind.

As nearly always happens in such cases, the symbol soon became the god. The original creed was lost and forgotten, the similarity and appropriateness of symbolism brought about further confusion, and the Phallus became a deity. The worship of the generative power was at first of the most pure and simple character, crude in manner, primitive in form, pure in idea, the homage of man to the Supreme Power, the Author of Life.

Afterwards the worship became more defined, more depraved, a religion of feeling, sensuous bliss corrupted by priests who were not slow to take advantage of this state of affairs and introduced profligate and mysterious ceremonies, unions of gods with women, religious prostitution, and other degrading rites. Thus it was not long before the emblems lost their primitive meaning and were replaced by licentious statues and debased objects. Hence we have the depraved ceremonies at the worship of Bacchus who became, not only the representative of the creative power, but the god of pleasure and licentiousness.

The corrupted religion always found eager votaries, willing captives to a pleasant bondage based on the impulse of physical pleasure, as in India and Egypt, and among the Phoenicians, Babylonians, Jews, and other nations.

Sex worship once personified became the supreme and governing deity, enthroned as the ruling god over all devotees to the shrine of Isis and Venus, Priapus and Bacchus, inspired by the most animating passion of nature.

Naturally the whole of the Triad or triangle symbolism could be used not only to express this Male-Female-Sex axiom, but also to express the new personification or god, the Phallus and his two natural attributes, Asshur, Anu, and Hea of the Assyrians, the Rod and Stones of the Ark, and the conjunction of this new triad with the female monad gave a new apparent interpretation to the tetrad.

This apparent meaning of ancient symbols is a snare ever set for the unwary, and many explanations have been given starting from the above-mentioned basis. The attempts of the supporters of purely sexual theories to explain the 'three in one ' mystery inseparable from any trinity result only in the introduction of a fourth term which no longer fits the case, or in the consideration of an obviously incomplete half-symbol.

All the older symbols seem complex at first sight, and as we trace out their history, their various forms and uses, we find a multiplicity of explanations as to their meaning. But this multiplicity is only apparent, and is due not so much to the fact that by its very concentration a symbol does represent several laws, but to the numerous interpretations

STONE STATUETTES OF THE REINDEER AGE

that have been given to it during the evolution of human thought and religious systems, wilfully by the priesthood, unconsciously by the people. Thus a symbol may well express a number of different creeds according to the period under consideration, and that explanation will be the true one that is most complete, oldest, and most universal, the common origin of the many systems it represents. We can consider the Cross, for instance, as the simplest and earliest expression of the tetrad, but if we were to confine our investigations to comparatively recent origins we might consider it as a direct derivation of the crux ansata, and its meaning would then be purely phallic. If it so happened that no record of history existed prior to the advent of Christ we should not hesitate in considering the Cross as the instrument by means of which Christ was put to death, and would most probably look for no further meaning.

The old symbols were adopted and retained for the very reason that they expressed both an abstract philosophical doctrine and an actual concrete natural law, and one or other of these interpretations came into pre-eminence according to the predominance of sexual worship or spiritual doctrines.

Nature to the early man was not brute matter, but a being invested with his own personality, and endowed with the same feelings and passions, and performing the same actions. He conceived the course of nature from the analogy of his own actions. Generation, begetting, production, bringing forth were his ideas of cause and effect.

The Earth was looked upon as the mould of Nature, as the recipient of seeds, the nurse of what was produced in its bosom. The sky was the fecundating or fertilising power.

'The Sky,' Plutarch says, 'appeared to men to perform the functions of a father, as the Earth those of a mother.' (Westropp, Phallim.)

The Phallus and the Cteis, the Lingam and the Yoni, the special parts contributing to generation and production, becoming thus symbols of those active and passive causes, could not but become objects of reverence and worship.

The indecent ideas attached to the phallic symbol were the result of a more advanced civilisation verging towards its decline, of which evidence may be found in Rome and Pompeii.

In other words the Phallic cult, from being primarily the symbol of an abstract doctrine, became not merely the deification of the generative function in man, but a widespread and universal Nature worship, the cult of fecundation, a natural religion deprived of its primitive demonology. Priapus became Hermes and Pan, god of gardens, god of nature, of the woods, and of the brooks, which were later peopled with nymphs and satyrs.

> 'L'eau sur ses bords invite la verdure,
> Et la verdure invite aux amours.'
> Desmoustiers.

The erection of such vast architectural masses as the Pyramids or the Tower of Babel, dating from the foundation of the Chaldean Monarchy by Nimrod, the son of Cush, 2221 B.C., was done with the object of setting up before the eyes of mankind the indestructible monument of a universal creed; but, subsequently, the corruption of human nature urging men to overthrow a spiritual worship which absolutely required purity and holiness, they sought to establish a system that virtually inculcated the worship of the creature more than the creator, and furnished a pretext for the practice of unrestrained licentiousness as part and parcel of religious rites, so that the lingam was the object really worshipped under its colossal representative in the Chaldean tower, though such structures were originally erected with a higher, more abstract aim.

'Whatever the Egyptians meant by the symbol in question, it was certainly nothing ludicrous or indecent, of which we need no further proof than its having been carried in solemn procession at the celebration of those mysteries in which the first principles of their religion, the knowledge of the God of Nature, the First, the Supreme, the Intellectual, were preserved free from the vulgar superstitions and communicated under the strictest oaths of secrecy to the initiated who were obliged to purify themselves prior to their initiation by abstaining from sexual intercourse and all impure food. We may therefore be assured that no impure meaning could be conveyed by this symbol, but that it represented some fundamental principle of their faith.' (Payne Knight.)

Moreover, there appear two distinct forms of Priapi at the origin, a fact which gives added weight to this argument. The primary Priapus was a personification of the great generative principle of the universe, the secondary Priapus, a personification of that particular generative faculty that springs from animal desire.

The Phallus and its emblems were representative of the gods Bacchus, Priapus, Hercules, Siva, Osiris, Baal, Asher, etc., who were all Phallic deities. Siva (Baal or Maha Deva) was not merely a reproducer of human forms, he represented the fructifying principle, the generating power that pervades the universe. The Symbol is always in his temples. It is usually placed in the inmost recess or sanctuary sculptured in granite, marble, or ivory, and often covered with flowers. Small images of this emblem carved in ivory, gold, or crystal are often worn as ornaments, the pious use them in prayers, and the devotees of Siva have it written on their foreheads in the form of a perpendicular mark, in the same way as the worshippers of Vishnu bear the maternal symbol as a horizontal mark.

Phallus signifies 'he breaks through' or 'passes into.' The word survives in the German 'pfahl' and 'pole' in English. Phallus is supposed to be of Phoenician origin, the Greek word Pallo or Phallo, 'to brandish preparatory to throwing a missile,' is so near in assonance and meaning to Phallus that one is quite likely parent of the other. In Sanscrit it can be traced to Phal, 'to burst, to produce, to be fruitful,' then again Phal is a ploughshare and is also the name of Siva and Maha Deva, the Hindu deities.

The emblems of the Phallus were poles, pillars, and stones, and the cults and deities which invariably accompanied Phallic worship were sun worship, serpent worship, and tree worship. We will examine each of these in turn.

We have said something concerning the erection of monoliths in the first chapter, but a great number of these are undeniably phallic in design and purpose, and are to be found in every country without exception. The Maypole is of phallic origin, and staffs and poles are frequently found as emblems of the Phallus. Pillars are very common in most countries, and are often at first clearly phallic in shape, till they finally take the form of towers, spires, and minarets. These various emblems of the Phallus are very common, and were the expression of the male or active principle.

The Yoni or Cteis was less frequently pictured for two reasons. It was the passive principle, and therefore considered to be less sacred, and it existed already in concrete form as nature, whereas the male principle (in its more general sense) was abstract. 'Mother Earth 'is a legitimate expression only of the most general type. Religious genius gave the female quality to the earth with a special meaning. When once the idea obtained that our world was feminine it was easy to induce the faithful to believe that natural chasms were typical of that part which characterises woman. As at birth the new being arises from the mother, so it was supposed that emergence from a terrestrial cleft was equivalent to a new birth. In direct proportion to the resemblance between the sign and the thing signified was the sacredness of the cleft and the amount of virtue imparted by passing through it.

From natural caverns being considered holy, the veneration for appertures in stones as being equally symbolical was a natural transition. Holes such as we refer to are still to be seen in those structures which are called Druidical, both in the British Isles and in India. It is impossible to say when these first arose, it is certain that they survive in India to this day. We recognise the existence of the emblem among the Jews in Isaiah xi. in the charge to 'look to the hole in the pit whence ye are digged' (Anacalypsis, p. 346). We find it also in the following Hebrew ritual, which is very significant and plays an important part in the explanation of the Sun-Myth. The womb of Ked or the Dolphin form of tabernacle was specially characterised by coverings emblematical of sun worship and the death of the sun and rebirth. The inner covering was purely astronomical, being designed with the signs of the Zodiac, and over that were dolphin's skins, and over that rams' skins dyed red to imitate flesh, ' the flesh of her nakedness.' At the east end of the tabernacle, the end of the Holy of Holies, the fabrics were looped into a cleft, out of which the sun was reborn. The High Priest clothed in all the life symbols, bells, and pomegranates, entered by the west at sunset on the 20th of December, and put on grave clothes and showed himself to the people as the dead sun. He then lay forty hours in the Holy of Holies till the morning of the 22nd, when he thrust himself through the dolphin-lined cleft and was 'born again' (Hannay, *Sex Symbolism in Religion*).

In modern Rome, in the vestibule of the church, close to the temple of Vesta, there is a large perforated stone, in the hole of which the ancient Romans are said to have placed their hands when swearing an oath, in imitation, or rather in counterpart, of Abraham swearing upon the male organs, 'place thou thy hand upon my thighs.'

The carving of the female organ and crude statuettes to be found over church doors and elsewhere in Ireland are further examples of the female emblems of the sex cult.

Male emblems, as we have seen, are far more frequent. As the male genital organs were held in early times to exemplify the actual creative power, various natural objects were seized upon to express the theistic idea, and at the same time point to those parts of the human form. Hence a similitude was recognised in a pillar, a heap of stones, a fig-leaf, a tree between two rocks, a club between two fir cones, a trident, a thyrsus tied round with two ribbons with the two ends pendent, a thumb and two fingers, the caduceous, etc. Equivalent to the Yod or Lingam we find Ab the father, Asshur, Anu, Hea, Abraham, Adam, Esau, Edom, Ach, Sol, Helios, Dionysus, Bacchus, Apollo, Hercules, Brahma, Vishnu, Siva, Zeus, Jupiter, Aides, Adonis, Baal, Osiris, Thor, Oden, etc. The Yoni or Cteis was represented by Isis, Astarte, Juno, Venus, Diana, Artemis, Aphrodite, Hera, Rhea, Cybele, Ceres, Eve, Frea, Frigga, the queen of heaven, the oval, the trough, the delta, the door, the ark, the ship, the chasm, a ring, a losenge, cave, hole, pit, celestial virgin, and a number of other names such as the shell, almond, pomegranate, moon, etc.

Both Sun Worship and Serpent Worship, two very important branches of religion, are subdivisions of the great Phallic or Nature cult. They resulted naturally and unavoidably from Phallic worship, and in some cases became separate and distinct religions.

Sun worship and serpent worship, all the gods and theurgies with which we are now familiar, arose from Phallic worship, and moreover, all the pre-existing symbols, gods, and theurgies were absorbed by and adapted to this cult. Phallic worship was both a worship of the great generative principle of the universe, of nature, and of that particular generative faculty of sex, but at its origin it was itself merely a symbol, a blind, a concrete prototype of a far older abstract creed, and it remained so, at any rate as far as the priests and initiates were concerned, for a considerable time. In other words. Phallic worship as a symbol was too striking, too near the truth, too inspiring in a physical sense to remain a symbol, and the image became the god.

Before we examine sun worship, the most important religious system directly derived from the Phallic cult, we will deal with serpent worship, which plays so great a part in religious symbolism and legend.

The true meaning of the snake symbol is not very clear, and the origins of, and reasons for, this cult involved and obscure because of their multiplicity.

The snake is a symbol of Wisdom, a symbol of Life, a symbol of Eternity, and a Phallic symbol. These various meanings do not appear at first sight to be compatible with one another. Certainly the oldest and simplest form of snake symbolism is the serpent biting its own tail, or symbol of eternity, the circle or cycle of life common to all religions and which we have already mentioned in a preceding chapter. From the earliest times the serpent has been connected with the gods of wisdom. It was the especial symbol of Thoth or Taaut, a primeval deity of Syro-Egyptian mythology, and of such gods as Hermes and Seth.

According to Sir Henry Rawlinson, the most important titles of this deity refer ' to his functions as the source of all knowledge and science.'

Not only is he the ' intelligent fish,' but his name may be read as signifying both life and a serpent. The serpent is the Sun god, Tonacatl-Coatl, the principal deity of the Mexican pantheon. Serpents are looked upon by African and American tribes as embodiments of their departed ancestors, and a similar notion is entertained by certain Hindoo tribes. It is evident, moreover, that we often find the idea of evil connected with the serpent god. The snake was not a direct phallic symbol. The original and most essential meaning was that of life, eternity, the perpetual cycle or flow of life. The association of the snake with wisdom arose in those countries where successive lives, or reincarnation, were held to be necessary before man could gradually raise himself from the baser state to that of purity and wisdom. The only way to attain wisdom lay through time, through the lapsing of a large number of periods or cycles, and perfect wisdom could only be attained through an eternity, the god without beginning or end as S5rmbolised by the serpent biting its tail. The universal conjunction of the ideas of perfect wisdom and eternity in the person of the principal deity substantiates this theory.

The phallic associations are a direct deduction from this idea since the notion of eternity, or cycle of life, was embodied in the fourth term of the tetrad, the term of transition, which was the very essence of continuation or eternity, and which was endowed with a productive, sexual, or phallic meaning.

Thus, not only is there nothing inconsistent in these three meanings of the serpent. Eternity, Wisdom, and Sex, but they appear naturally connected by their common emblem the snake.

The reasons why the snake was chosen for such an emblem arc fairly obvious. Although by no means intelligent, it appears wise, the suggestion of continuity afforded by a coiled serpent biting its own tail, or even by the mere notion of a snake, is obvious. In addition it is Phallic in form.

We find further substantiation for this opinion if we consider the relative frequency and antiquity of the three meanings. Our data consists of the fact that innumerable examples demonstrate the existence of the three meanings. Beyond any doubt the Eternity meaning is the most frequent of the three, while between the two others there is little difference. When we consider the question of antiquity we again find that the Eternity meaning is the oldest, the other two seem to have appeared simultaneously. We can therefore safely conclude that both the Wisdom and Phallic interpretations were derived from the emblem of Eternity. Time or Eternity being the necessary condition for perfect wisdom, and the generative or reproductive function being the necessary condition to ensure a continuation, a repetition of the cycle of life, which is the true sense in which the word Eternity should be taken. The common factor or meaning of these three entities can be taken as *Continuity*, the continuity of time, the continuity of acquired knowledge, the continuity of life. So that we may more appropriately state that the Snake was the emblem of Continuity. If we accept this meaning, the apparently varied instances of snake symbolism, far from being inconsistent, are seen to be the logical expression of a common thought, to be at unison in aim and meaning, and a further corroboration of our original basic theory. In that very remarkable work, *The Rivers of Life*, Forlong traces back religious systems to a number of distinct original creeds, the Sun, Fire, Phallic cult. Serpent worship, Tree worship, and Ancestor worship.

We already know that if we accept the trinitarian doctrine as being the origin of religious systems. Phallic cult, and as we shall show, both fire and ancestor worship are the logical results of its evolution, while sun, serpent, and tree worship are merely elaborations of the Phallic cult, a point which many authors have fully demonstrated as regards sun worship.

In other words, the multiplicity of origins is removed at

ARDANARI ISWARA.

TYPICAL BI-SEXUAL FIGURE, WITH SNAKE AND LOTUS SYMBOLS

once. That one or other of these secondary cults should have become predominant in such or such a country is only natural, and we must also bear in mind the ever-present tendency for the symbol to dethrone the god, for the concrete picture to replace the abstract idea. It is through this tendency that sects arose whose' worship was true, unsymbolical, direct serpent worship, sun worship, or tree worship, to the confusion of superficial investigators. Sun worship, as we have already seen, was a direct consequence of Phallic worship, though in some cases it actually pre-existed, but merely as a part of natural demonology, there being a demon or spirit attached to the sun.

When first the idea of duality arose, the sun naturally became the emblem of the spirit, of the active and fecundating principle, while the moon became the emblem of nature, of the passive or female principle. The connection between the seasons of the year and the fecundation and gestation of nature must have been obvious to the most primitive minds, and the sun was the true emblem of that more comprehensive Phallic cult that embraced nature as a whole, while the Phallus remained the emblem of a narrower form of the same cult.

This can be expressed by stating that the sun or sun god was the primary Priapus, the god Pan, while the cult of the actual generative powers of man, or secondary Priapus, was the symbol of a symbol, a narrower, more material doctrine, the true origin of lustful practices and insincere religions, of the cults later connected with Bacchus.

I hope at some later time to devote a further volume to the study of this point, but I feel I have already said more than is compatible with the scope of these essays. The reader will wonder what bearing these considerations have on the subject of this work, and my answer is that the importance of symbolism is so great that we cannot hope to understand the meanings and far less the origins of Sorcery, Black Magic, and Magic proper without its help, and in order to understand those primary principles that are so wonderfully expressed in the old symbols we must make a careful examination of the original creeds that are the foundation of religious structures and the guiding factor in the evolution of human thought. I must bid the reader be patient. Though half these essays are devoted to the study of the growth of human thought, when we come to examine the arcanas of occult science we shall find that we have gathered on our apparently round-about way a master key to those mysteries over which superstition, credulity, and ignorance have kept an uninterrupted watch from the very dawn of civilisation.

In this chapter we have considered the esoteric aspect of Phallic worship and the various forms of its symbolical expressions rather than its practical or ceremonial side, to which a great many writers have devoted volumes. It is necessary for our purpose, however, that we should get a clear impression of the Phallic ceremonies of the past, and we will consequently conclude this chapter with a number of examples taken from the practices of the more important sects.

Before passing on to these let us sum up briefly the conclusions we have reached. Phallic worship is twofold, and consists of a lustful cult of the generative function of man, which is but a corruption or symbol of a broader cult, the cult of the fecundating and begetting properties of nature, the cult of the sun. This double entity is in itself only the symbol or concrete form and material interpretation of the abstract trinitarian creed. The Phallic cult, being the exact counterpart of an abstract and subjective creed, it follows that such symbols and deities as were originally devised to express the latter are also perfect expressions of the former, with the result that religious systems throughout the world, after they have progressed and risen from the Phallic stage, maintain a symbolism, ceremonial, and deities which are apparently purely and solely Phallic in origin.

The Phallic cult is common to all nations and religions, but there is very sound evidence to prove that it was by no means a primary form of worship, and, moreover, in a great number of cases it did not come into being for a considerable time. Before the Romans invaded Gaul, and while Druidic cults remained pure and untainted by foreign practice, the worship of human forms or animal forms was entirely unknown to that country. The worship of Priapus was imported by the Romans.

The first statues or anthropomorphic gods set up by the Gauls and Celts bear out this statement very markedly. The statue of a woman, of very great antiquity, to be seen at the Chateau Quempili, in Brittany, is provided with a long scarf, the ends of which effectively veil the sex. A statue of Hercules bears an ample lion skin carefully drawn over the sex, and several statues of the god Mercury which were found on Mount Donon, between Alsace and Lorraine, though naked, are remarkable from a phallic point of view; the sex is in all cases hidden under a belt or entirely absent.

This reserve, however, was not of long duration, and both Gauls and Celts followed the Roman lead; but it is quite certain that no form of Phallic worship existed in Gaul before the conquest by Caesar.

It should be remembered, of course, that Phallic worship always showed a stronger tendency to develop in warm Eastern or Southern countries, and that it was connected to a certain extent with the culture of the vine. The East and South, moreover, had reached a much higher degree of civilisation or evolution. But this is by no means without exception. Both the Swedish and Saxon religions developed a complete sun and Phallic cult in a combined form long before the era of Roman influence.

Of the two main forms of Phallic worship which we have defined, the worship of the Phallus proper was confined to the people, while the priests and more enlightened members of the community were more exclusively sun worshippers, considering the sun as the true upholder of life. As Hannay very truly points out, these early religious systems were highly solar in their conception and highly Phallic in their practical worship.

The Hebrew religion, founded on older symbols and derived by Moses from Egyptian teachings, is entirely Phallic in form. The Rod of God as described in the Old Testament is certainly Phallic, and the Testimony, or holy stones, were the equivalent of the Hea and Anu of the Assyrians. These stones were afterwards called the Tables of the Law, but the names 'testimony' and 'witness' are certainly Phallic. The method of swearing in those days was as Abraham commanded his servant, 'Put, I pray thee, thy hand under my thigh.' This form of oath is still in existence today among the adepts of certain initiatic societies. We must here remember that it is not the man who swears who is the witness, although that meaning has crept in in modern times, it is the things upon which men swear that remain as the witnesses to their promise. So God gave Moses two stones or testes to put into the ark, or female symbol, together with the Rod or Phallus.

The fact is commented upon by Dr. Ginsingburg in Kitto's *Cyclopedia* thus: 'This practice evidently arose from the fact that the genital member, which is meant by the euphemistic expression thigh, was regarded as the most sacred part of the body, being the symbol of the union in the tenderest relation of matrimonial life, and the seat whence all issue proceeds and the perpetuity so much coveted by the ancients. (Compare Gen. XLVI. 26; Exod. I. 5; Judges vii. 30.) Hence the creative organ became the symbol of the creator and the object of worship among all nations of antiquity. It is for this reason that God claimed it as a sign of the Covenant between Himself and His chosen people in the rite of circumcision.'

A great portion of the facts have been suppressed by the translators, who have given to the world histories which have glossed over the ancient rites and practices of the Jews.

Forlong says: 'It should not be, but I fear it is, necessary to explain to mere English readers of the Old Testament that the Stone or Rock Tsur was the real old God of the Arabs, Jews, and Phoenicians, that this would be clear to all Christians were the Jewish writings translated according to the first ideas of the people and Rock used as it ought to be instead of God, Theos, Lord, etc.'

The Jews, like the Phoenicians, had the same rites and gods as the surrounding people, and the entire Christian religion as we understand and practise it today is of Phallic origin. The whole story of the life of Jesus and His position of Saviour, even including every detail and incident of His life, pre-existed in Asia under various other names for thousands of years before the Christian era. Such figures as Krishna were identical to Christ, and the whole history of these periodical Saviours or initiates is an elaborate symbol in itself, the apparent meaning of which is that of the annual sun, his lowly birth in winter, his struggles with the cold, stormy January and February, his passover or cross-over at the spring equinox when by crossing over the equator and ascending into the northern half of the skies he ensures the salvation of mankind from the deadly cold of winter. But there is as always a deeper meaning to these Saviours of history, these 'dying gods,' as Fraser terms them, which I will deal with in the chapter on initiations. However, the Saviour episodes that occur in all religious systems may be taken primarily as being expressions of the Sun-Myth. Hannay has very clearly expressed this point. A list of twenty-six Saviours can be given before Christ with quite identical histories as to the main features. In the case of Krishna there are sixty-two coincidences, while thirteen incidents are different, and these refer to fishes, and there is little doubt that the Romans introduced sun worship at a time when there was a change of sign in the Zodiac in which the sun dwelt at the spring equinox. The change was from lamb to fishes. Twin worship was universal about 6000 B.C., when the sun was in Gemini, and the names were for ever after held sacred. About 4500 B.C. the sun passed to Taurus, and we get the sacred Bull Nanda in India, the man-headed winged bulls of Assyria, the worship of the cow Hathor in Egypt, and of

Apis the Bull. The slow shifting of the earth's axis known as the precession of the equinoxes caused the bull to pass away from the position of the sun's house at the spring equinox and the ram took its place. We have then the Ram or Lamb symbols, and finally about the time of Christ it passed into pisces or fishes, hence the fish miracles in the New Testament and fishermen disciples.

In other words the sun god was given as a personal emblem that sign of the Zodiac which happened to correspond to the position of the sun at the spring equinox. According to the invariable rule, in a great many cases the image dethroned the god, and so certain sects or tributary worships arose whose gods were Twins, Bulls or Cows, Rams, etc.

Generally speaking. Phallic rites and ceremonies can be divided into two groups that correspond to the two forms of the cult, the sun or nature cult, and the Priapic or pure Phallic cult. In the first group we find rites and ceremonies connected with spring, and the fecundation of nature, our harvest festival being a direct descendant of this type, and in the second we find ceremonies of a more lustful nature, such as the celebrations of Bacchus, while there is yet another series of rites that are more exactly a survival of Phallic rites, those connected with the images and deities that were supposed to influence fertility in women.

In India the Phallus and Cteis were called Lingam and Yoni, and the combination of these forms the altar in the greater number of Hindoo places of worship, a cup-shaped structure from the centre of which rises a column.

The various Hindoo temples contain paintings of various Phallic objects or towers and upright columns consecrated to the Lingam, while the celebrated shrines of the Jagrenat and Elephanta contain groups of figures which cannot be described. The usual rites connected with fertility are practised either in the form of offerings to the Lingam or by actual sexual contact with a consecrated image or amulet, or with priests, while religious prostitution is common, as, indeed, it was in all countries. Phallic worship in India is interesting on account of its prevalence and on account of its extraordinarily crude and open form. Religious art in India is quite undisguisedly phallic, and no attempts have been made to moderate its symbols or the expressions of their variety.

In ancient Egypt the Phallus was a highly honoured object. Phallic images were to be found in all the temples, and were carried in solemn processions into the surrounding country during the feasts that were celebrated in honour of Osiris.

Herodotus gives the following description: –

'The Egyptians celebrate the feast of Bacchus very much as the Greeks do, but instead of a Phallus, they carry images about one cubit in height which can be set in motion by means of a cord. The women carry these images from town to town, the procession being led by musicians and singers.'

Among the Greeks and Romans the worship of Priapus was very conspicuous, and the Bacchic and other ceremonies almost identical in form to those found in Egypt or India. The procession was led by naked girls, and these were followed by a number of virgins carrying golden baskets full of the first plucked fruits and flowers, among which lay some tame snakes and Phallic images crowned with flowers. Next came the Phallophori, men dressed in long robes, crowned with ivy, and bearing great poles or staffs hung with phalli. These were followed by musicians singing and crying, 'Evohe Bacche, lo Bacche.' Behind these came the Ithyphalli dressed in women's clothes and staggering as though drunk. Groups of satyrs and girls, semi-naked and bearing torches or the thyrsus, pranced around performing erotic dances, while the satyrs led rams to be sacrificed. These processions invariably ended in orgies of drink and unbridled sexual excesses.

The Romans called the feasts of Bacchus, Bacchanalia and Liberalia, because Bacchus and Liber were the names of the same god, although the feasts were celebrated at different times of the year and in a somewhat different manner. The latter were celebrated on the 17th of March with the most licentious gaiety when an image of the Phallus was carried in triumph. These festivities were more particularly celebrated among the rural or agricultural population who, when the preparatory labour of the agriculturist was over, celebrated with joyful activity nature's reproductive powers which in due time were to bring forth the fruit.

During the festival a car was drawn along containing a huge Phallus, and the worshippers indulged in obscene songs and dances of a wild and extravagant character. The gravest and proudest matrons suddenly lost all decency and ran screaming through the woods half naked with dishevelled hair interwoven with pieces of ivy or vine.

Similar enthusiastic frenzy was exhibited at the Lupercalian feasts instituted in honour of the god Pan (under the shape of a goat), whose priests ran naked through the streets on the morning of the festival striking the married women they met on the hands or body, which was held to be an omen of promising fertility.

Further examples of these rites will be given in the chapter concerning the Sabbat; to give any more here would be mere repetition.

The Phallus is still a common talisman in Italy. At Isemia in the eighteenth century these symbols were offered for sale quite openly, being a palm in length and sacred to St. Cosmo and St. Damian. The Phallic cult in Europe continued down to the fifteenth century, though denounced at Le Mans in 1247 and at the Synod of Tours in 1396, the time at which the first Sabbats were appearing in Italy and France. As late as the last century the festival of Palm Sunday in certain parts of France bore a Phallic name and Phallic symbols were used and carried in procession. A similar practice existed at St. Jean d'Angely, where small cakes were made in the form of a Phallus and carried in procession at the Fete-Dieu.

We see the Phallic cult thus gradually fading out, and the sects that maintained its more licentious forms broke away, as we shall see in a later chapter. We can readily understand how in more enlightened days, when a certain reserve and prudery had developed among civilised people, Phallic worship in its cruder forms could not continue to flourish, and religion, in order to maintain its dignity and power, began to eliminate Phallic worship and everything connected with it.

CHAPTER V

THE DEVIL-MYTH AND BLACK MAGIC

'We shall be saved through the flesh.'

Black Mass Ritual.

The study of religious symbolism, although I have been compelled to restrict myself to a statement of the main outstanding facts, has shown us that religious systems were built up from a fundamental subjective trinitarian creed for which a more objective form was later substituted. Phallic worship in its broadest sense. But the law of balance, the conception of soul and matter on which this original creed is based, led to a singular misinterpretation. We are now no longer dealing with the objective prototype of a subjective conception, we are faced with an altogether different scheme, a duality of opposition, in which the bond is one of hatred and rivalry. The original creed is a complementary duality, the other a duality of opposition.

It was my intention originally to entitle this chapter 'The Devil-Myth' and to leave aside all questions connected with Black Magic to be dealt with in a later chapter, but I find that these two subjects are so intimately connected, so identical, that it is impossible to keep them apart. The Devil–Myth must naturally find its place here as the second great ramification derived from the idea of duality, and Black Magic equally naturally emerges from it, although it is somewhat out of place in a chapter preceding that on Sorcery.

The new dual system originated in the conception of opposition, the opposition of a principle of good to a principle of evil, of a dark god to the god of light, and, although it occurred in, or spread to, every religious system, it is comparatively recent and may be said to have originated in its true form with Manes and the Manichean sect. Manes was born in a.d. 216, and Manicheism survived till the fifteenth century, but the influence of this terrible creed was such as to modify and corrupt the whole of religion, turning it into a thing of terror, in which the idea of God was effaced by the presence of an ever-lurking monster and a lurid Hell.

This concrete idea of a Devil or evil god did not arise all at once, and only gradually took shape.

The old traditions of natural demonology provided the first substance for this materialisation. Early civilisations certainly had a demon or demons of evil among the spirits of their materialistic theurgies, but they were incidental, one of many, very different from the ' great adversary of mankind.' The Greeks, for instance, had no Devil in the true sense of the word, the evil spirits found in mythology are part of the main demonological scheme; the Eumenides and Harpies are examples of these.

The first appearance of a more concrete form of demon or angel of evil occurs at the time when the Zoroastrian doctrine became known among the Hebrews. In later Judaism and the

New Testament Satan appears as the Prince of Evil Spirits (Ephes. ii. 2), the opponent of the Kingdom of God, and consequently a copy of Ahriman and his Dews in opposition to Ormuzd. Satan does not appear in any writings before the period when the Jews became familiar with the Persian faith. For example, we are told that the Lord, not Satan, hardened the Pharaoh's heart against Israel (Exod. vii. 13), and again God, not the Devil, hardened the spirit of Sihon (Dent, n. 30. Conf. Jos. xi. 20). (Inman.)

When we carefully examine the use of the word Satan in the Old Testament we find some remarkable facts. Satan is described as ' Adversary ' in Num. xxii. 22, 32; in I Sam. xxix. 4; 2 Sam. xix. 22, 23; in i Kings v. 4 (18); and in xi. 14, 23, 25. Now according to these texts we find literally that ' an angel of the Lord ' is Satan, that David might become Satan if he went to light, that Abishai and Joab were satanic, that Hadad the Edonite, Rezon the son of Eliadad, were both Satan, whilst if we turn successively to 2 Sam. xxiv. i and i Chron. xxi. i we recognise the astounding fact that Satan and Jehovah were identical. After this it is nothing to find that Peter, the rock upon which the Christian Church is said to have been built, was designated Satan by his master (Matt. xvi. 23). Incongruities like this may readily be multiplied: for example, Gen. XXII. I, ' God did tempt Abraham,' or the Lord's Prayer, ' Lead us not into temptation.' These apparent discrepancies may be reconciled by comparing Jehovah and Satan to the Hindoo Siva, who is both creator and destroyer.

In other words, throughout the Bible God is described as a sort of Bifrons, having a gentle mien and loving heart to all who believe, but a countenance and mind full of fury, vengeance, and persecution towards those who presume to disbelieve. In fact, Moses himself describes the Almighty, or His angel the pillar of cloud as being double-faced, a cloud of darkness to the Egyptians, but a bright light to the Hebrews (Exod. xiv. 20). (Inman.)

There is nothing in this conception of Satan approaching the more recent Devil, the diabolical personage of Goethe, for example, the monster of the Middle Ages. We merely find here a tendency to group together those factors that were inimical to man coupled with a natural egotistical desire that the tribal god should support his chosen people against their enemies, a very similar idea to the German conception of God during the war.

When the religion was more essentially monotheistic, like that of the Hebrews,[1] the evil occurrences such as war, defeat, illness, plagues, natural cataclysms, were provided for by the very nature of God which was that of a powerful but entirely human being who could be angry and avenge himself, or loving and kind, a superhuman ruler far more than a God, and there was no need for a prince of darkness or Devil.

In essentially polytheistic systems, on the other hand, the personified principles of evil, anger, jealousy, vengeance found their place quite naturally among the deities of the existing demonologies, and here again there was no place for a spirit of evil as a separate powerful entity.

---

1   Some writers having translated 'Elohim' as 'the Gods' instead of Lord in the Old Testament have concluded that the Hebrew religion was really polytheistic. This is incorrect. Elohim does not mean 'the gods', but 'Him, the Gods.'

The legends, the material, the minor deities were there, however, and only needed the formulation of a creed of opposition to become part and parcel of it.

An examination of the Talmud shows that the first idea of a true Devil as opposed to God, a god of evil, arose from the dualistic theology of Zoroaster. We find in the Avestas continual antagonism between Ahoura-Mazda or Ormuzd, god of wisdom, and the Angramanyou Ahriman, the malevolent, the god of evil. This god of evil was surrounded by demons or Dews. But the Mazdeism of Zoroaster was not a religion of opposition in the same sense as Manicheism, although Manes based his dogma partly on these old principles. He indeed it is who can be said to be the true originator of the Devil; if it had not been for the poison of his pernicious doctrine Satan would have been merely an impersonal natural phenomenon instead of becoming the horrifying spectre of Christian theology.

The antagonism between the two principles of duality was older than even Zoroaster, and can be traced back to the earliest traditions of India. This old Hindoo tradition tells us that at the beginning of all things the genii of the North and those of the South quarrelled about the beverage of immortality, both sides desiring the exclusive use of this elixir. Long and disastrous wars resulted in the defeat of the southern genii or Assours, who were enslaved to the northern genii or Devas. This tradition also exists in the Edda of the Scandinavians, and was known to the Egyptians, Greeks, and Romans as the war of the gods and giants.

From a duality of opposition, from the paradoxical conception of a god of evil perpetually antagonistic to a god of bounty arose that formidable entity, the Devil, As we have seen, there was sufficient tradition, legend, and similar minor deities to provide him with a numerous consort of demons, while the idea of punishment for sin, or symbolical houses of pain, which in original religions stood for the successive lives of the individual better or worse according to his actions, provided ready material for the elaboration of his domain or Hell.

It is our object in this chapter to follow the growth of the monster from his vaporous origins to his almost concrete reality and to bring out the pernicious results of the introduction of this idea into religious systems. Black Magic and the greater part of Sorcery are directly derived from this idea, while the repulsive and grotesque conception of the Devil and the inconceivable injustice of eternal damnation proved fatal to the strength and development of Christianity, although the Church found it, no doubt, a powerful weapon at first.

We first find spirits and demons connected with natural demonology combined with the belief in certain definite evil spirits, such, for example, as those demons which arose from the legendary intercourse of Adam with a female spirit, Lilith, and of Eve with a male spirit, Sammael, the oldest trace of the Incubus and Succubus which I shall deal with in a later chapter, or the fallen angels, punished for their connection with the daughters of man, as described in the Book of Enoch. Certain other partial myths such as Beelzebub, Python, Asmodeus, Belial, Lucifer, and Shatan all embodying some sort of belief in an evil force or forces, combined again with the above, give us about the third century b.c. a more or less mythical, indefinite entity of evil inimical to man. During His life Christ, finding some rudimentary idea of a Devil or evil influence amongst the Jews, makes use of it as a symbol to illustrate His teachings.

The third century a.d. brings us to Manicheism, to the idea of a good and an evil god, and Black Magic was an immediate result of this or similar doctrines. With the spreading of Christianity about the fifth century, the various evil principles in existence in other religions were taken up and used as a basis and foundation for the creation of the Devil.

The Devil is first defined at the Council of Toledo in 447, and the Council of Constantinople in 547 bestows upon him the gift of immortality. The monster is born; he has taken definite shape, he is become a true entity, officially consecrated, a lurking horror, a roaring lion ever ready to devour, and the Christian religion has become a creed of terror, while other religions the world over are suffering from the same influence, but to a lesser extent.

Manicheism was one of the most important attempts to found a universal religion and to reconcile the Christian, Buddhist, and Mazdeen with Greek philosophy. It presented the same syncretic ideas found later among Moslem Druzes and among Sikhs. It failed in the first place because Islam presented a much simpler system in the East, and because in the West Christianity was already developing, in the time of Manes, a religion which aimed at reconciling the Paganism of Italy and Gaul with the ethics of Christ, this presenting a simpler and more familiar faith. But the one achievement of Manes was the creation of the Devil which led to an afterwards unremovable taint throughout religion. Manes was a notable philosopher and religious teacher born about the year a.d. 216, and he was crucified and flayed alive by the Persian Magi under Bahram I in the year A.D. 277. His Persian name was Shuraik, rendered Cubricus in Latin. He was of high birth and a native of Khbtana. His Acta Archelei became the Manicheen Bible with sundry added epistles. He taught the Mazdeen dualism of the powers of light and darkness, as representing good and evil beings, and an asceticism which aimed at the control of all passions. Manes repudiated Judaism, and, Uke the Gnostics, regarded Jehovah as an evil God. The Manicheens were more hated and feared by Catholic Christians than any other sect. They were still in existence in spite of constant persecution as late as our tenth century, and their influence was felt from China to Spain and Gaul. It still lingers in Asia, and among the ' Christians of St. Thomas ' in Madras it survived till the fifteenth century. St. Augustine had listened for nine years to Manes, but the Roman Empire felt the force of this system chiefly in a.d. 280. The Romans knew it themselves in a.d, 330, and Faustus became its missionary among them. Many clung to Manicheism till A.D. 440, when Leo the Great found that he must stamp it out if the Roman creed was not to be extinguished. It was the basis of the Paulican heresy, and of that of the Albigenses in the South of France which was only quenched by blood in the thirteenth century (Forlong.)

The doctrine of Manes can be summed up as follows. He believed in two gods, or, more exactly, principles, the principle of good and that of evil. Before the creation of the world the 'people of darkness' revolted against the God, and God, incapable of withstanding the attack, gave to them a portion of His essence. The people of darkness having within them the principle of evil by their very nature, and the principle of good which they had just acquired, were able to constitute the world, where both these principles are combined, but where the principle of evil predominates as the natural characteristic of its originators. Man is a mixture of two natures, the spiritual being the work of God, the body, and especially sex, the work of the Devil.

Manes and the Manicheens disappeared for reasons quite unconnected with Christianity. From certain standpoints their theories were a direct menace to social life, and were therefore very strongly persecuted by the emperors and others. From Manicheism proper sprung innumerable sects at various times and in various countries. In reality these various sects were inconsistent and rapidly vanished. Their devotees divided themselves into two distinct classes; the first, consisting of those disciples who believed in the predominance of the good principle, gradually drifted back into Christianity; the second, consisting of the believers in the predominance of the evil principle, turned towards the Shatan of antiquity and from that moment the mystic, uncertain, vaporous myth of the Devil took shape, waxed, and grew.

It soon possessed its dogmas, lithurgies, devotees, and churches. The monster was alive, he was effective and real, while within the Church the gradual elaboration of Hell and its horrors was preparing a fitting domain for the Prince of Terrors.

The Hell of Christianity was brought into official existence by the Council of A.D. 547, and it is from that date only that we find any mention in prayers or writings of the descent of Christ into Hell.

The belief in the Devil was curiously popular. Faced with an irresistible and semi-divine force of evil which God Himself could not entirely conquer, man felt his responsibility as regards sin considerably relieved. Satan became in a way the scapegoat of human vice and depravity.

Mankind, moreover, has always found an unhealthy pleasure in feelings of terror or fright, and the fear and terror connected with the Devil was intensified and carefully developed by the Church, who quite rightly recognised and appreciated its worth at a time when the attractions of Phallic worship were fading into the background.

The Devil and Hell, curiously enough, were not developed simultaneously, nor did they arise from the same origins. Whereas the Devil was born from the duality of opposition, Hell was derived from the idea of reincarnation, from the houses of pain, or fives of suffering which became the portion of the wicked after death. Hell was conceived as the counterpart of Heaven, so the Devil, becoming naturally king in Hell, a god opposed to a god, Christianity unconsciously fell into the Manicheen error.

Sorcery, as we shall see in the next chapter, was already rampant, both in the East and in Greece, where divination, philters, charms, necromancy, etc., were rapidly developing.

Sorcery (we must here necessarily anticipate somewhat on the subject of the next chapter) was mainly a veil for crime. But sorcerers and their like followed no definite system. Their practices were based on vague traditions, the knowledge of animal and vegetable poisons, and some rudiments of crude science. In order to enable them to grow into something more, a bond was missing, a universal leader, a god, and the old Satan reborn and glorified by the Manicheen sect, enthroned in Hell as the god of evil by the Church itself, proved to be the Messiah for which they were waiting. Under his guidance Sorcery assumes an entirely different aspect, and flourishes anew under this fresh impulse. From being more particularly confined to the peasantry and the ignorant, it spreads to all classes of humanity; from an agglomeration of fallacious superstitions held together by uncertain legends it becomes a dogmatised doctrine, a systematic religion, and the terrified consultants of countryside sorcerers and witches become the frantic devotees of the shrine of Evil.

First and foremost amongst these manifestations of what has now become Devil worship we find the Black Mass or Devil Masses of the Middle Ages, from which the ceremonial and ritual of Black Magic are derived. The principle which forms the very essence of the Devil, the idea of opposition, also underlies the whole ceremonial and ritual of Black Magic and Black Masses. Such ideas as repeating prayers backwards, reversing the cross, consecrating obscene or filthy objects are typical of this sense of opposition or desecration, which is also a recognised form of mental disease. The keyword to the whole of the practices of Black Magic is desecration, a tendency which exists in a very subtle form and happily latent state in a great many individuals of quite normal temperament. The old symbolism which had been carefully retained both by religion generally and initiatic societies was taken up by these sects in reversed form. The pentagram was the form universally employed by Devil worshippers, reversed with its point downwards, the symbol of a universe governed by passion as opposed to intellect, and the probable origin of the goat or ram, the Devil's most familiar form. There were other reasons why the Devil should be thus pictured, of course, the ram being in any case a symbol of divinity, and the sexual aspect of the same symbol proving an important factor in the matter. The satyrs of antiquity were not so very different in form from the Devil of the Middle Ages, the expression of malignity is absent, but the bestiality and lust persist.

The first forms of Black Mass were comparatively simple and free from the rites which rendered the later ones so famous. They died out in the seventeenth century, and were the remains of the practices of sects derived from and surviving Manicheism, celebrated not in honour of Satan alone, but in honour of Satan and God, good and evil. The priest was dressed in black, the time midnight, the ornaments of the altar three black books and three skulls, and parts of the service were reversed. Instead of 'The word was made flesh,' 'The flesh was made word,' or, ' We shall be saved through the flesh,' etc.

This form of ceremony belongs more properly to the Manicheic sects than to the domain of Black Magic. It is the transition form, the first step. There was more to come.

There seem to have been two influences at work, both of which contributed equally towards the introduction and development of true Black Mass.

The first is a renaissance of Phallic worship, or rather the desire of woman to take part in religious ceremonies as of old, from which she had been banished from the early days of the Church (an example of a similar motive is to be found at the root of the doctrine of the Christian Scientists). Woman became the priest, she later became the altar and the offering, and through this adjunction of the sexual element the Black Mass obtained its peculiar atmosphere. The second influence was that of the remains of Pagan sacrificial rites to be found in those remote places where the dissident sects were driven by persecution. Animal victims and human victims were offered to strange gods, and these rites were incorporated into the ceremonial of Black Masses and, in those days of perpetual famine, many were the devotees who attended these ceremonies in order to partake of the flesh of the sacrifice.

Thus do we enter into a new phase, the phase of blood, the 'Messes Sanglantes' of sinister fame. These rites and ceremonies spread from the country to the towns, from moors to secret closets, and from there to the courts. We have the horrors connected with Giles de Rais (Bluebeard); we have the Blood Mass celebrated before Charles IX of France to know whether in after life the massacres of the Protestants would be recorded as a crime against him. The king was lying on his death-bed, and a young child, after undergoing those rites which the Church ordains for communion, was brought in at midnight. On an altar, over which hung the image of Satan treading on the cross, a renegade priest consecrated two wafers, a white and a black one. The white wafer is given to the child, and on the instant his head is severed from his body and placed on the black wafer when the words 'Vim Patior' seem to come from his lips.

From that moment the Black Mass has come to stay. The Bishop Gilles Lefranc, Davot, Mariette, Lesage are all ardent devotees. The ceremonies become more sexual in form, sadism appears, and the details of these celebrations, interesting though they are in fact, do not bear putting into words. The most celebrated women are connected with them. The Marchioness d'Argenson, the Duchesses of Bouillon, of Saint Pont, of Luxemburg, of Vendôme, and many others besides. Sorcery and crime, sadism and Satanism, sexual and scatological practices grow and spread; we are in the presence of Black Magic proper, the ceremonial, systematic form of Sorcery, based on the deification of Satan.

This is the time when Pacts or agreements with the Devil make their appearance, examples of which are very numerous. On some specimens preserved to this day in museums or private collections the signature of the Devil appears as a black mark or scratch, occasionally burnt or scorched around the edges.

It should be remembered that throughout all this period of the Middle Ages there was only one strong body in authority, namely, the Church. The King was a distant star as far as his people were concerned. His barons and nobles were continually fighting one another, and the population of the country was a prey to armed bands of retainers and passing troops. There was no justice, no safeguard. In order to restrain the passions of humanity under such conditions the Church made use of the Devil and the fear of Hell, and took great pains that he should seem very real and become an object of terror for all. Unfortunately, if he was easy to raise he proved impossible to lay, and the remedy was worse than the disease.

Towards the beginning of the seventeenth century the Devil had become an ever-present menace. Any mysterious happening was his doing; he was the explanation of all mysteries. One could not open a book, take a step, speak a word without coming across him. He was all-pervading, and led the world. Such a state of things, such conditions of continual abject superstition and terror, answered the sorcerers' purpose in a way they had not dared to hope for, and they were not slow to use the opportunity. So bad did matters become that the king is obliged to open the 'Chambre Ardente' in France, a special tribunal to deal with Satanism, and ladies and nobles of the court of France are involved in the cases brought before it.

Some traces of Black Magic are to be found in comparatively recent times. As late as 1855 an association of women was discovered in France, the members of which, partaking of Communion several times a day, retained the wafers in their mouths till they could transfer them to some container where they were stored and afterwards used in various forms of Satanic rites. In 1874 again women were employed for the purpose of collecting consecrated wafers and given large sums of money for the wafers obtained.

In Agen, in 1843, a secret society was discovered that had been celebrating Black Masses for years. It was found that over three thousand consecrated wafers had been used in this way. Not many years ago there existed a certain Comte de Lautrec who used to send the churches gifts of statues and ornaments which he had previously cursed and dedicated to Satan.

Cases of the same sort are to be found at the present day, and Black Masses are still undoubtedly celebrated in the larger capitals of the world.

In some respects the rites of Black Magic closely resemble the Sabbat, and are a form of sexual hysteria mingled with

Phallic religion. Black Magic is merely a glorified form of Sorcery in which the Devil is invoked, and which is extremely ceremonial in form. Herbs and ointments, as well as drugs, are used to provoke visions in much the same way as we shall describe in the chapter dealing with the Sabbat.

It is difficult to realise, and the fact cannot be too strongly stressed, the all-pervading satanic atmosphere of the Middle Ages, and if this is clearly understood then that particular branch of the occult known as Black Magic will appear in its true light. It was not an opposition to White Magic, though in some cases it was certainly an abuse of the ceremonial and practices of that doctrine with an evil object in view. An interesting sidelight on this aspect of Black Magic will be given when we come to examine the practices connected with Magic initiation. But the real fundamental principle of Black Magic is exposed when we examine the origins and development of the Black Mass which was indeed the ' grand oeuvre ' of that pernicious belief. The alliance of Sorcery with this satanic worship, and the alliance of these with sexual depravity and hysteria give us the peculiar forms and aspects of a belief that to this very day holds terrors and mysteries for those who give it but a superficial examination.

It was based on the Devil, on the existence of a divinity of evil, which could be worshipped and served, and which would serve in return, and in this form it was neither mysterious nor dangerous, except to the participants themselves, for such collective mystic ceremonies where drugs were burnt or absorbed quickly lead to a contagious form of hysteria, while epilepsy and insanity were rampant. The devotees of the black art would have been no more dangerous than the drug fiends or sexual perverts of today had they not also been expert poisoners. Such women as the Voisin and the Brinvilliers were adepts in Black Magic, and rank among the most famous poisoners the world has ever known.

There is nothing in Sorcery but crime and ignorance. There is nothing in Black Magic but the free indulgence of religious and sexual insanity, which are very closely allied, and it flourished in the Middle Ages on account of the advent of the Devil. It still exists at the present day, with its gatherings of sexual perverts, sadists, drug fiends, all those who stand on the borderline of insanity, to worship that quintessence of human vice and depravity, the Devil.

In earlier days God was an impersonal abstract being, inhuman and un-understanding, but the Devil was an individual whose thoughts and desires were similar to ours, frightening, perhaps, but obliging, and the temptation was very great. He offered love, money, power, the belief in the possibility of such things was universal, and men, young and old, and women even signed pacts and lived thereafter with the haunting fear of their impending doom, a doom which from the descriptions of the Church was horrible beyond words. Can we wonder that it took very little to persuade such people as these, weakened as they were by fear, to lead them slowly from perversion to perversion, from crime to crime, along the road to insanity in the hope of forgetting even for an instant that eternal damnation that must have seemed far worse to them than any crime they might commit.

If the Church had declared 'there is no Hell, the Devil is a myth' Black Magic and all similar practices would have died out of their own accord, they were not compatible with

a healthy state of mind. But as we know the Church needed
something to scare the people into some form of discipline
and order, and if it had disavowed the Devil it would have lost
its grip. Which of the two would have proved the lesser evil is
a very doubtful question.

CHAPTER VI

SORCERY AND WITCHCRAFT

*'La sorcellerie est la negation de la raison, le triomphe de
la betise, du desequilibre, et du crime.'*

Eliphas Levi.

SORCERY I have defined as a collection of practices based
on tradition, superstition, and a crude form of science.
Where the wise acted with discernment, the ignorant jumped
to conclusions, and the facts and coincidences observed by
science became the laws and doctrine of the sorcerer.

Sorcery has its origin in demonology; while the priest-
rulers of the tribes strove to rule with justice and discernment,
the sorcerers aspired to power and achieved their object
by trading on the fear and superstitions of the people.
Demonology was distorted to suit their purpose, and picking
up what crumbs of knowledge they might gather in their
ignorance, they ruled through fear and suggestion, preying
on the criminal or lustful tendencies of their devotees.
Amongst the tribes of Africa and other primitive people of
the world the witch-doctor plays a very prominent part; on
close examination it will be found that the general trend

of the means at his disposal and the effects he can produce are identical with that of the sorcerer of Thebes, Rome, or the Middle Ages. Amongst such tribes as still retain a crude and bestial demonology, with prominent Phallic rites and sacrificial ceremonies, the sorcerer and priest merge into one. This is to a very great extent the case of tribal communities in Africa and elsewhere; in very primitive tribes there is no duality, the sorcerer and priest are one, and the duality is a later product of evolution, the witch-doctor becoming a separate entity.

The lore of Sorcery is rich, its history long and intricate. Its unhealthy influence can be traced in many unexpected quarters, and few cults are truly free from its taint. The more ignorant the individual, the more credulous he becomes, and the more prone to believe in the fearful and satanic nature of the many things that pass his comprehension. Stupidity and wickedness are boon companions, and the man who has failed will resort to foul means if he cannot triumph by fair.

Sorcery consists of so great a number of practices, and the unbounded credulity of the darker ages has so contributed to its complication and elaboration, that it would be hopeless to attempt a description of any but the more outstanding forms. These, however, are remarkable on account of their similarity the world over, and the frequency with which they occur. They can be considered as the mainsprings of Sorcery, and if we add a knowledge of plant and animal poisons, a strong criminal instinct, and a shrewd mind we will have reduced Sorcery to its constituent parts.

These practices are based on what Doctor Fraser has termed Sympathetic Magic, the belief that acting on one object will have an effect on another if there is a similarity between them, or if there has been contact between the two. Here again the term Magic has led to confusion; such practices have, of course, nothing whatever to do with Magic proper, although their counterpart is to be found in certain of its rites. These homoeopathic and contagious practices, the true purpose and meaning of which we cannot really grasp until we have examined White Magic, form the basis and occult foundation of Sorcery. They are to be found in another form and with an entirely different significance in Magic, and their prevalence in Sorcery is due to a corruption of those practices in Magic. It is quite difficult to draw a line between Sorcery and Black Magic, and these practices are really limit cases between the two. In other words. Sorcery proper has no true occult aspect beyond the superstitious fear with which the sorcerer used to impress his victims and the simpler homoeopathic and contagious practices distorted by tradition. Whenever these practices assume a more elaborate or ceremonial form they merge into the domain of Black Magic. The main distinction lies in the fact that whereas the adept of Black and White Magic acts in accordance with a regular and well-defined system, the sorcerer is an ignorant being for all his malevolence, and blindly carries out imperfect and corrupt instructions obtained by oral tradition or from the many written Grimoires. The magician believed in his art and was in deadly earnest, consequently he was very rarely dangerous. The sorcerer, on the other hand, quite clearly realised the absurdity of his practices, he was. essentially fraudulent, and the sway he held over mankind was proportionately greater.

The most common of these practices is the attempt to injure or destroy other human beings by the injury or destruction of an image of the victim. These images were usually made of wax, and the likeness was made as perfect as possible (homoeopathy). In many cases the figure was draped in some garment or part of a garment which had at one time been worn by the victim – hair, finger-nail parings, etc., were collected and added to the figure, which was then mutilated or destroyed. Notwithstanding the very curious experiments which were carried out in France in the latter part of the last century on hysterical patients in two Paris hospitals, and granting that these experiments contained no hidden source of error, we have absolutely no facts to prove or reasons to believe that such practices were based on anything but the crudest superstition. In a later chapter, when defining what I have termed Magic Initiation, we shall find a possible connection between purely magical beliefs on the one hand and the practices just described on the other.

Another familiar form of this performance consisted in following the victim secretly and driving nails or thorns into his footprints. The terror which the discovery of such an action inspired in the mind of the victim was often sufficient actually to cause his death. There are innumerable examples of such happenings even in comparatively modern times. A variation of this idea consisted in spitting on or otherwise defiling a person's shadow.

The early Priest-Kings of humanity certainly used a form of Sympathetic practice to propitiate the divinities and obtain rich crops or fertile wives. Many examples of this are to be found in all the earlier religious systems, and it has been suggested by S. Reinach in *Art and Magic* that the drawings of animals that are to be found in the cave dwellings of prehistoric men served the same purpose. His deduction lies on the observation that in no single case do we find a drawing of a carnivorous or savage animal, all the paintings depict edible animals such as the bison or reindeer. In the same way certain carved statuettes found in these caves and representing exceedingly fat and swollen females do not suggest to my mind 'that their women kind must have been obese,' as some writers have stated, but I think it far more probable that they should have been intended as charms against barrenness and sterility. So obvious is the attempt to make them fat and swollen that it cannot be solely due to the artist's lack of skill.

Another important feature of Sorcery was the phenomenon of bilocation. Sorcerers were believed to be able to haunt and worry their victims in their own homes, though they remained invisible and were in reality found asleep in their own beds when investigations were made. The various and as yet unexplained phenomena due to hypnotism proper, self-hypnotism, and mediumistic clairvoyant trances give us some sort of a key to the true nature of so-called bilocation. We will return to this subject, however, in a later chapter.

The bible of the sorcerer was the Grimoire, a collection of absurd recipes with which almost everyone is familiar. There are many of these in existence, some harmless, others particularly obnoxious and dangerous. In order to show up Sorcery in its true light it may be of interest to quote a few extracts from these compilations.

A most admirable method of curing a drunkard. Take two live eels and enclose them in a jug of wine till they are dead. Let them stand in the wine for three days, after which time they may be removed. If the wine thus prepared be served to a drunkard at dinner he will be cured of drinking for ever. (We are quite prepared to believe in the efficacy of this remedy.)

To stop any snake. On seeing him, pronounce the following words, Osi, Osoa, Osia, and he will be helpless in your hands.

To stop one or several people. Say Veide, Rongan, Rada Bagabin, bend on one knee, put the right wrist on the ground, and rise up again.

To see at night. Rub your face with the blood of a bat and you will see at night as clearly as in the daytime.

To see that which is invisible to others. Take the excretions of a cat and the grease of a white hen, mix these together, and rub the mixture over your eyes.

These few examples which have been chosen quite at random should be sufficient to show how little importance can be attached to Sorcery. Many of the instructions given in these collections are totally imprintable.

But the knowledge of vegetable and animal poisons, however, and the use of aphrodisiacs opened up for Sorcery the unlimited fields of crime. It is really far more on account of crime as the inseparable companion of Sorcery that Witchcraft was so persecuted in every country and at every period.

Sorcery proper was really nothing more than a school for crime, a ready means of making a living by preying on the credulous fears of the ignorant. The sorcerer would communicate some illness to a man's cattle, or to the man himself, and, when consulted, would declare that a spell had been cast, and would offer to remove it for a consideration. If a man had an enemy to remove the sorcerer was called upon to brew those vegetable poisons with which he was familiar, while disappointed lovers and jilted maids bought inoffensive drugs or, more often, powerful aphrodisiacs.

In those savage tribes where the witch doctor is an entity of some importance his art consists almost entirely of similar criminal practices. Crime and the exploitation of human vices and passions is the keynote and *raison d'être* of Sorcery.

The practices of Sorcery were universally condemned all over the world. The Harris Papyrus, discovered in Thebes in 1855, gives us confirmation of this, and contains curious facts concerning Sorcery in Egypt. Mr. Chabus deciphered the remains of another papyrus from the same source in which we find an account of the trial and condemnation to death under Ramses III of a shepherd for the crime of Sorcery. All religions and legislatures have condemned Sorcery as a crime. Plato mentions a law of death for Sorcery, and Demosthenes describes the case of the witch Lemnia. Pausanias gives us an account of a special court of justice established in Athens for the suppression of Sorcery. In Rome the Leg. Duodecim Tabularia, articles 55, 68, and 69, punish with the death penalty all such practices, and we fed that one hundred and seventy sorcerers were put to death during the Consulates of Claudius Marcellus and Valerius Flaccus. Under Augustus two thousand books dealing with Sorcery were publicly destroyed in Rome.

The Salic Law (a.d. 496) mentions the crime of Sorcery as a capital offence. Chilperic III in the early part of the eighth century published an edict against Sorcery, and in Germany in the latter part of the same century (a.d. 772) Charlemagne founded the Sainte Vehme for the suppression of these same practices.

No chapter in the forensic history of the world, however, could equal that which may some day be written concerning the witch trials of the Middle Ages. In order to appreciate the true nature of this extraordinary episode it is essential to grasp the main stipulations of the legal code that was especially devised at the time for the purpose. From the summary which is given below it will apparent that the result was not merely the suppression of Sorcery, but the creation of a state of perpetual suspicion and unrest wherein no individual was safe from arbitrary arrest, torture, and death. Here are some aspects of these witch laws as applied in the Middle Ages and to which we will return in the next chapter.

Public rumour or an anonymous denunciation was sufficient to justify immediate arrest; no privilege of age, sex, or rank could be considered; sons were allowed to give evidence against their fathers, daughters against their mothers. A single witness was sufficient to ensure conviction; in no case could torture be omitted, 'an excellent procedure in the case of a young girl, a child, or a delicate woman.' (This quotation is verbatim.) In all churches urns were placed where anonymous denunciations might be deposited; the reason for arrest was in no case revealed to the victim, and no acquittal pure and simple could be given.

The clergy was responsible for these drastic amendments, and in France, in the year 1281, an act of parliament turned over to the Church the legislative power for such crimes. This act was not repudiated till the fifteenth century.

The number of victims, as might be expected, was enormous. In Lorraine, Nicolas Remigius burned 900 victims, the Bishop of Geneva in 1596 burned 700 victims in less than six weeks; Grillandu, the inquisitor of Arezzo (1520), admitted over 2000 victims, while Sprenger and Pierre de Lancre and many others counted in thousands. All over Europe witch-finders and the like arose in countless numbers. Their favourite method consisted in sticking long pins into the victims' bodies, and should a spot be discovered that was not sensitive to pain they were found guilty and burnt; in either case they were tortured and executed.

Crimes connected with Sorcery may be divided into three main types. The first type of crime is that committed by the dupes of an unhealthy curiosity or an inordinate vanity, who dream of riches or of mastering other men by means of some form of supernatural power. The second type includes all those crimes due to jealousy and envy, hate and the desire for vengeance, and crimes committed for the sake of evil. Thirdly, we find a series of crimes committed by beings who have been led away by the greed of avarice or the promptings of disordered and perverted sexual desires. The famous case of Gilles de Rais is a typical example of this last type. In such cases Sorcery proper is so mixed up with other practices, such as alchemy and Black Magic, that it is very difficult to find the line of demarcation.

Religious communities and convents have contributed their share to the lore of Sorcery, and have often been afflicted with possession, a great number of these cases being found in the records of history. It is but another case or phase of sexual disorder brought about by long abstinence and confinement, and the Sorcery trials of the times refer to a number of such cases. In one particular instance the nuns were seized by convulsions which spread rapidly to the whole community. The victims raved and mumbled unintelligible words, and accused two priests of having cast spells upon them, one of these priests, Bouille, was alive, the other, Ricard, had been dead for over a year. The nuns of Sainte Beaume, the Ursulines of Ludun, and others have furnished memorable examples of these disorders. In the famous case of Urbain Grandier we find a poor priest whose unfortunate indiscretions with a nun result in a whole convent having convulsions. One and all accuse him of Sorcery, and after a long trial and the most horrible tortures, though nothing can be proved against him, he is condemned to death and burnt at the stake.

These examples show us two categories of cases, the ones due to criminal sexual perversion (..es de Rais), the others due to the hysterical ravings of sexually tormented communities. Such forms of contagious hysteria are well known to modern medical science. But there is also, as we know, a third and larger category, cases of actual practised Witchcraft, of which we find innumerable examples.

Some ignorant but ambitious or jealous peasant dabbles in medicine, rudimentary science, and the extravagant nonsense to be found in the Grimoires, his neighbour would perhaps be taken ill and die, and the coincidence would prove his undoing. Public rumour would fill in the details according to approved traditions, and a new case of Sorcery would be added to the records of the local law courts. Let us examine a typical case taken from the Justiciary Records of the seventeenth century.

The shepherd Hoque was brought to trial on account of a strange epidemic that had spread among the cattle. Public rumour accused him, and he was arrested and duly charged. He was found guilty and condemned to hard labour. In spite of this, however, the epidemic did not abate, and in order to discover his secret a companion was given to Hoque in his prison while he was awaiting his transfer to the galleys. This spy wormed himself into Hoque's confidence, and the shepherd confessed that he had buried in a stable which he described an evil charm and that the epidemic could only die out on its destruction. This news was conveyed to the parliament, the charm duly found and destroyed. The epidemic stopped, but the records add that Hoque died in horrible pain the very instant the charm was burnt.

This example is peculiar in form and interesting for that very reason. Readers will find innumerable examples in works dealing with this phase of the occult which space will not allow me to quote. I propose, however, to conclude this chapter with the account of a number of really typical cases. The first one combines nearly every form of phenomenon pertaining to Witchcraft. The extraordinary nature of the accusations and the incredibly flimsy evidence on which the death sentence is obtained are very characteristic, and when we consider that the whole of the facts connected with Sorcery are of this nature we can understand how unreal and devoid of foundation any belief in such phenomena must be, the frequency of their occurrence being entirely due to the very nature and severity of the laws promulgated against them.

The second case is really an anticipation on the subject of the next chapter, but the interesting lights thrown on the mechanism of justice in such cases justify its inclusion here.

I have left them both in the original English for reasons which the reader will readily appreciate, and they will be found appended at the end of the present chapter.

Sorcery can therefore be split up into the following component parts. Firstly, a survival of ancient demonology in its cruder and more primitive forms. Secondly, the misapplication of distorted scientific laws. Thirdly, a misconception and totally unreasonable use of what Fraser has termed Sympathetic Magic. Fourthly, an accumulation of traditional medicine, the knowledge of plants and vegetable poisons, and the use of drugs. Fifthly, divination of a sort. These component parts were bound together by tradition and superstition, and their true raison d'etre was the perpetuation of crime in some form or other. A history or complete description of Sorcery and its numerous forms and variations does not come within the scope of these essays; I have had to rest content with the few typical examples given, showing that it is an entity in itself independent of, and entirely different from. Magic Initiation. There is an intermediate stage, a hybrid doctrine, belonging to neither and partaking of both – Black Magic. We may conclude that although in some cases sorcerers or witches may have possessed mediumistic powers, where the phenomena produced are very similar to those described in modem seances, the sorcerer throughout history held no kind of supernatural powers whatsoever.

His apparent power and very real influence he derived from the fear which he instilled into the minds of the ignorant masses already imbued with legends and superstition, and only too ready to believe. The only effects he produced were due to direct suggestion and autosuggestion of his victims and his criminal use of poisons and drugs from which he drew the greater part of his profits. Divination was a necessary adjunct to his art, and the curative value of plants was well known to him. Necromancy he sometimes practised, but this belongs more properly to the domain of Black Magic.

The sorcerer was a dispenser of poisons and drugs, and in every sense of the word an evil-doer. His powers were directly proportional to the credulity of his victims and thus we find him flourishing in the darker and grosser epochs of history; and the true adepts of Sorcery were almost entirely confined to the country, away from towns and centres of education, where the simpler minded peasantry afforded, and still afford, him the opportunities required.

Occasionally we find him attached to the fortunes of the nobility; he even boasted at times of Royal patrons; he became a true poisoner, a more subtle type of bravo whose crimes left no traceable clues. But at the best he was a criminal, a coward, and a charlatan, shunned by all, envious and evil-minded, trading on the basest instincts and impulses of the human race.

The more grotesque the formulae, the more preposterous the mixture, the more effective they appeared to his distorted mind. He distilled in his retorts the mould collected from the skulls of corpses hanging in the gibbet chains. The animal kingdom gave him its venoms, the vegetable kingdom its drugs and poisons, and, an object of terror to all, an irreconcilable enemy of mankind, he was to be found bending over his unhealthy brews, chanting sacrilegious and obscene incantations, an object for loathing and ridicule.

Case I

The trial of Julian Cox which containeth the witchcraft of Julian Cox and her trial.

Julian Cox aged seventy years was indicted at Taunton in Somersetshire about summer assizes 1663 before judge Archer then judge of assizes there for witchcraft which she practised upon a young maid.

For the proof of the first particular the first witness was a huntsman who swore that he went out with a pack of hounds to hunt a hare, and not far off from Julian Cox's house he at last started a hare. The dog hunted very close, and the third ring hunted her in view till at last the huntsman, perceiving the hare almost spent and making towards a great bush, he ran on the other side of the bush to take her up and preserve her from the dogs, but as soon as he had hands on her it proved to be Julian Cox who had her head grovelling on the ground, and her globes (as he exprest it) upward. He knowing her was affrighted that his hair on his head stood on end, and he spake to her and asked her what brought her there But she was so far out of breath that she could not make any answer, his dogs came also up with full cry to recover the game, and smelt at her and so left off hunting any further. And the huntsman with the dogs went home presently sadly affrighted.

Secondly, another witness swore that as he passed by Cox's door she was taking a pipe of tobacco upon the threshold of the door, and invited him to come in and take a pipe, which he did. And as he was taking Julian said to him, 'Neibourg, look what a pretty thing is there.' He looked down, and there was a monstrous great toad betwixt his legs staring him in the face. He endeavoured to kill it by spurning it but could not hit it. Whereupon Julian bid him forbear, and it would do him no harm; but he threw down his pipe and went home, which was about two miles off Julian's house. He told his family what had happened and that he believed it was one of Julian Cox's devils. After, he was taking a pipe of tobacco at home and the toad appeared betwixt his legs; he took the toad out to kill it and to his thinking cut it into several pieces; but returning to his pipe the toad still appeared. He endeavoured to burn it but could not. At length he took a switch and beat it. The toad ran several times about the room to avoid him, he still pursuing it with correction. At length the toad cried and vanished, and he was never troubled with it.

Thirdly, another swore that Julian passed by his yard while his beasts were in milking, and stooping down scored upon the ground for some small time. During which time his cattle ran mad, and some ran their heads against the trees and some of them died speedily. Whereupon concluding they were bewitched, he was after advised of this experiment to find out the witch, viz., to cut off the ears of the bewitched beasts and burn them, and that the witch would be in misery and could not rest until they were plucked out. When he tried, and while they were burning, Julian Cox came into the house raging and scolding, that they had abused her without a cause, but she went presently to the fire and took out the ears that were burning, and then was quiet.

Fourthly, another witness swore that she had seen Julian Cox fly into her own chamber window in her full proportion, and that she very well knew her and was sure it was her.

Fifthly, another evidence was the confession of Julian Cox herself, upon her examination before a justice of the peace which was of this purpose that she had been often tempted by the devil to be a witch but had never consented. That one evening she walked out about a mile from her own house and there came riding towards her three persons upon three broomsticks borne up about a yard and a half from the ground two of whom she formerly knew which were a wizard and a witch that were hanged for witchcraft several years before, the third person she knew not. He came in the shape of a black man and tempted her to give him her soul, or to that effect, and to express it by pricking her finger and giving her name in the blood in token of it, and told her that she had revenge against several persons who had wronged her but could not bring her purport to pass without his help. And that upon the terms aforesaid he would assist her to be revenged against them. But she said she did not consent to it. This was the stun of the general evidence to prove her a witch.

But now for the second particular to prove her guilty of the witchcraft upon the maid whereof she was indicted; this evidence was offered.

It was reported that Julian Cox came for an alms to the house where this maid was a servant and that the maid told her she would have none and made her a cross answer that displeased Julian whereupon Julian was angry and told the maid she would repent it before it was night. And so she did for before night she was taken with a convulsion fit and after that left her she saw Julian following her and cried out to the people of the house to save her from Julian.

However none saw Julian but the maid, and all did impute it to her imagination only; and of the night she cried out of Julian Cox and the black man that they did come upon her bed and tempted her to drink something they offered her, but she cried out and defied the devil's drenches. This also they imputed to her imagination and bid her to be quiet because they in the same chamber with her did not see or hear anything and they thought it had been her conceit only.

The maid the next night, expecting the conflict she had the night before, brought up with her a knife and laid it at her bedhead. About the same time as the night before Julian and the black man came again upon the maid's bed and tempted her to drink that which they had brought but she refused crying in the audience of the rest of the family that she defied the devil's drenches, and took the knife and stabbed Julian, and as she said, wounded her in the leg and was importunate with the witness to ride to Julian's house presently to see if it were not so. The witness went and took the knife with him; Julian Cox would not let him in, but they forced the door open, and found a fresh wound in Julian's leg as the maid had said, which did suit with the knife and Julian had just been dressing it when the witness arrived. There was blood also found upon the maid's bed.

The next morning the maid continued her outcries, that Julian Cox appeared to her in the house wall and offered her great pins which she forced her to swallow. And all the day the maid was observed to convey her hand to the house wall and from the wall to her mouth, and she seemed by the motion of her mouth as if she did eat something. But none saw anything but the maid, and therefore thought still it might be her fancy; and they did not much mind it. But towards night the maid began to be very ill and complained that the pins which Julian had forced her to eat out of the wall did torment her in all parts of the body that she could not endure it, and made lamentable outcries of pain. Whereupon several persons being present the maid was undressed and in several parts of the maid's body several great swellings appeared and out of the head of the swellings several great pin points appeared which the witnesses took out, and upon the tryal there were about thirty great pins produced in court all which was sworn by several witnesses that they were taken out of the maid's body as in manner aforesaid.

Judge Archer who tried the prisoner told the jury that he had heard that a witch could not repeat the Lord's Prayer viz. 'and lead us not into temptation' and having the occasion he would try it; and told the jury that wether she could or could not, they were not in the least measure to guide their verdict according to it because it was not legal evidence; but that they must be guided in their verdict by the former evidence given upon oath only.

The prisoner was called for up to the next bar in court and demanded if she could say the Lord's Prayer? She said she could and went over the prayer readily until she came to that petition. Then she said, 'and lead us into temptation ' or 'and lead us not into no temptation,' but could not say 'and lead us not into temptation,' though she was directed to say it after one that repeated it to her distinctly but she could not repeat it otherwise than is expressed already; although tried it near half a score of times in the Open Court.

After which the jury found her guilty, and judgement having been given, within a few days she was executed without any confession of the fact.

Case II

Of the strange witchcraft discovered in the village of Mohra in Sweedland taken from the Public Registrar of the Lords Commissioners appointed by his Majesty the King of Sweden to examine the business in 1669-1670.

The news of this witchcraft coming to the Bong's ear, his Majesty was pleased to grant the appointement of commissioners, some of the Clergy and some of the laity to make a journey to the town aforesaid and to examine the whole business and accordingly the examination was ordered to be on the fifteenth of August and the commissioners met on the first in the said village at the parson's house; to whom both the minister and several people of fashion complained with tears in their eyes of the miserable condition they were in and therefore begged of them to think of some way whereby they might be delivered from their calamity. They gave the commissioners very strange instances of the Devil's tyranny among them. How by the help of witches he had drawn some hundreds of children to him and made them subjects to his power; how he hath been seen to go in a visible shape through the country and appeared daily to the people; how he had wrought upon the poorer sort by presenting them with meat and drink and this way alluring them to himself with other circumstances to be mentioned hereafter. The inhabitants of the village added with very great lamentations that though their children had told all and sought God very earnestly by prayer, they were carried away by him and therefore begged the Lords Commissioners to root out these witches that they might regain their former rest and quietness; and the rather because the children which used to be carried away there in the country of Elfdale since some witches had been burnt there, others remained unmolested.

That being the last Humiliation day instituted by authority for the removing of his judgement, the Commissioners went to Church, where there appeared a considerable assembly both of young and old. The children could read most of them and sing psalms, and so could the women, though not with very great zeal or fervour.

There were preached two sermons that day, in which the miserable case of those people who suffered themselves to be delivered to the devil was laid open; and those sermons were at last concluded with fervent prayers. The public worship being over, all the people of the town were called together to the parson's house, near three thousand of them. Silence being commanded the King's Commission was read publicly in the hearing of all and they were charged under very great penalties to conceal nothing of the truth; those especially who were guilty that the children might be delivered from the devil's clutches; they all promised obedience; the guilty feignedly but the guiltless weeping and crying bitterly.

On the fourteenth August the Commissioners met again consulting how they might withstand this dangerous flood.

After long deliberation, an order coming also from His Majesty they did resolve to execute such as the matter of fact could be proved upon examination being made. For there were discovered no less than three score and ten in the village aforesaid, three and twenty of which freely confessed their crimes and were condemned to die. The rest, one pretending that she was with child and the other denying and pleading, were sent to Fahluma where most of them were afterwards executed.

Fifteen children who likewise confessed that they were engaged in this witchery died as the rest. Six and thirty of them between nine and sixteen years of age who had been less guilty were forced to run the gauntlet; twenty more had no great inclination and yet had been seduced to those hellish enterprises, because they were very young were condemned to be lashed with rods upon their hands for three Sundays together at the church door, and the aforesaid six and thirty were also deemed to be lashed in this way once a week for a whole year. The number of seduced children was about three hundred. The examination was conducted as follows.

First the commissioners and the neighbouring justices went to prayers; this done the witches, who had most of them children with them which they either had seduced or attempted to seduce, were set before them. Some of the children complained lamentably of the misery and mischief they were forced to suffer sometimes of the witches. The children being asked if they were sure of being at any lime carried away by the devil, they all declared they were begging from the commissioners that they might be freed from that intolerable yoke.

Hereupon the witches themselves were asked whether the confessions of these children were true and admonished to confess the truth that they might turn away from the devil unto the living God, at first most did very stiffly and without shedding tear deny it though much against their will and inclination.

After this the children were examined every one by themselves to see whether their confessions did agree or no; and the commissioners found that all of them did punctually agree in the confession of particulars.

In the meantime the Commissioners that were of the Clergy examined the witches but could not bring them to any confession all continuing steadfast in their denials, till at last some of them burst out into tears and agreed to what the children had said.

The confession which the witches made to the judge in Elfdale agreed with the confessions they made at Mohra, and the chief things they confessed consisted in these points. Whither they used to go; what kind of place it was they went to, called Blockula; where the witches and devils used to meet; what evil or mischief they had either done or designed there.

I. Of the journey to Blockula, the contents of their confession: –

We of the province of Elfdale do confess that we used to go to a gravel pit which lay hard by a cross way and there we put on a garment over our heads and then danced round, and after this we went to the cross way and called the devil thrice. First with a shrill voice, the second time somewhat louder, and the third time very loud with these words, 'Antecessor come and carry us to Blockula ' whereupon immediately he used to appear, but in different habits; but for the most part we saw him in a grey coat and red and blue stockings; he had a red beard, a high crowned hat, with linen of divers colours wrapt about it and long garters upon his stockings.

Then he asked us whether we would serve him body and soul, if we were content to do so, he set us on a beast which he had there ready and carried us overhead, and after all we came to a green meadow where Blockula lies. We must procure some shavings of altars and some church clocks; and then he gives us a horn with Salve in it wherwith we do annoint ourselves and then he gives us a saddle with a hammer and a wooden nail therby to fix the saddle where upon we call upon the devil and away we go.

Those that were in the town of Mohra made in a manner they were sure of a real personal transportation and whether they were awake then when it was done; they all answered in the affirmative and that the devil sometimes laid something down in the place that was very like them; but one of them confessed that he did only take away her strength, yet sometimes he took even her body away with him.

For their journey they said they made use of all sorts of beasts, men spits, posts, according as they had an opportunity. If they do reide upon goats and have many children with them, that all may have room they stick a spit into the anus of the goat and then are anointed with the aforesaid ointment.

After the night, the children are exceeding weak, and cannot recover themselves the next day, and this happens to them in fits. And if a fit comes upon them they lean upon their mothers' arms, who sit with them up sometimes all night. They become pale and swoon, which swoon lasteth sometimes an hour, sometimes two, and when the children come to themselves again they mourn and lament.

II. Of the place where they used to assemble called Blockula, and what they did there.

They unanimously confessed that Blockula is situated in a delicate large meadow whereof you can see no end. The place or house they met at had before it a gate painted in divers colours. Through this gate they went into a little meadow distinct from the other where the beasts were that they used to ride on. But the men whom they made use of during their journey stood in the house by the gate in a slumbering posture sleeping against the wall.

In a huge room of the house they said there stood a long table at which the witches did sit down. And that hard by this room was a chamber where there were lovely and very delicate beds. The first thing they said that they must do at Blockula was that they must deny all and devote themselves body and soul to the devil and promise to serve him faithfully and confirm all this with an oath. Hereupon they cut their fingers and took their blood to write their names in his book. They added that he caused them to be baptised, too, by such priests as he had there, and made them confirm the baptism with fearful oaths and imprecations. Hereupon the devil gave them a purse wherein there were shavings of clocks, with a stone tied to it which they threw into the water and then were forced to speak these words, 'As these shavings of the clock do never return to the clock from which they are taken may my soul never return to Heaven.' To which they added blasphemy and other oaths and curses. After this they sat down at a table, and those that the devil observed most were placed next to him. But the children must stand at the door, where he himself gives them meat and drink. After meals, they went to dancing and in the meantime swear and curse most dreadfully, and afterwards sexual intercourse followed.

Those of Elfdale confessed that the devil used to play to them upon a harp and afterwards go with them that he liked the most into a chamber and he commited venerous acts with them. And this indeed all confessed that he had carnal knowledge of them and that the devil had sons and daughters that he did marry together and bring forth toads and serpents.

They said they had sometimes seen a very great Devil like a dragon with fire round about him and bound with an iron chain, and the devil that conversed with them told them that if they confessed anything he would let out that great devil upon them, whereby all Swedenland shall come into great danger.

III. Of the mischiefs and evil which the witches promised to do to man and beasts.

They confessed that they were to promise the devil that they would do all that's ill, and that the devil taught them to milk which was in this wise: they used to stick a knife in the wall and hang a kind of label on it which they drew and stroked, and as long as this lasted the persons they then have power over were miserably plagued and the beasts they milked that way till sometimes they died of it.

A woman confessed that the devil gave her a wooden knife wherewith going into houses she had power to kill anything she touched with it; yet there were few that would confess that they had hurt any man or woman. Being asked whether they had murdered any children, they confessed that they had indeed tormented them but did not know whether any of them had died of those plagues.

The minister of Elfdale said that one night he felt a pain as if he were tom with an instrument they cleanse flax with or a flax comb; and when he awakened he heard somebody scratching and scraping at the window but could see nobody. And one of the witches confessed that she was the person that did it, being sent by the devil.

An old woman of Elfdale confessed that the devil had helped her to make a nail which she struck into a boy's knee, of which stroke the boy remained lame for a long time.

The Lords Commissioners were indeed very earnest and took great pains to persuade them to show some of their tricks, but to no purpose; for they did all unanimously declare that since they had confessed they found that all their witchcraft was gone and that the devil was very horrible.

Among titles of other cases we find the following, which need no further comment: –

'How two Priests of Seventy years old, being unclean with the devil in the shape of a woman, were afterwards burnt.'

'How a boy of Bilson suspected of witchcraft for making black water, was watched and seen to squeeze ink into his water.'

'How a French peasant in France was a-travelling, the devil came riding by on horseback, asked the peasant if he would ride, so the peasant was glad of the opportunity, and he carried him up in the air and dropped him in Turkey so that he was forced to walk home to France again on foot.'

After reading the foregoing narratives, the reader will have appreciated the wonderful unconscious *naïveté* and humour to be found in them. There is an almost unlimited number of such cases, all of which have many points of quite remarkable interest.

CHAPTER VII

THE WITCHES' SABBAT

'*Et Ieurs pas ébranlant les arches collosales*
Troublent les morts couchés sous le pavé des salles.'

Victor Hugo.

During that particularly interesting period, the Middle Ages, sex worship, Sorcery, and Devil worship combined in a number of countries to produce a peculiar form of manifestation, the Sabbat. The Justiciary Records of all countries about this period are so full of details and accounts of Sorcery and examples of the Sabbat, and such was the publicity given to witch trials and the importance and number of these that to the average reader today the words Magic or Witchcraft conjure up visions of this episode alone in the long and elaborate history of human thought and its perversions.

In those darker ages education was non-existent, learning confined to the very few, but from the upheavals of this period civilisation and science later emerged. We are dealing with an unsettled epoch, when human thought was striving for freedom, when science was in its infancy, and regarded as a very fearful thing. Superstition and Sorcery were rampant, and religion in the minds of the people a creed of fear and terror which left them little hope for mercy. I have shown in a preceding chapter how the Devil-Myth arose from the world-old system of balance and analogy, and similarly a misinterpretation of the original symbols led to the exclusive worship of sex. These are the two governing principles of the Sabbat.

The true religion of the Middle Ages was one of fear and consequent tendency to propitiate the Devil. The divinity of darkness played a far greater part in the life of men than the more abstract idea of God. The teachings of the Church gave every encouragement to this idea. Corrupt though it was at the time, the Church was powerful; excommunication was a very real punishment and amounted practically to death by starvation. In order to retain this power and influence the safest method of dealing with uneducated minds was through fear. The lurid descriptions of Hell and of the tortures awaiting the damned, the idea of an ever-lurking Devil waiting for victims, the legion of minor demons over which he ruled, all of which we find in the sermons and religious writings of the time, accompanied by great wealth of detail, were the soil-preparing factors for the seeds of Superstition, Sorcery, and exaggerated sexual cults. The crop was a rich one. The Church itself became frightened at the result and at its own inability to control events, which showed a marked return to the sexual heresies of early days, but with a criminal character they had not hitherto possessed. The Bulls of Innocent VIII in 1484, of Alexander VI in 1494, Leo X in 1591, and Adrien VI in 1522 are proofs of the Church's efforts to strangle its obnoxious offspring. We have already seen that the number of victims was considerable, but in spite of this the evil was never entirely stamped out, and the Devil has remained to this day a very real being to many.

The victims were in the vast majority of cases women, and apart from the admitted prevalence of women amongst the adepts of Sorcery, evidence points to the fact that a great number of the later witch trials were due to a form of sadic indulgence.

There is an extraordinary similarity between even the smaller details to be found in accounts of the Sabbat or other manifestations of the same kind derived from the confessions of participants alleged or otherwise. This similarity exists moreover not only between the confessions obtained in any one district, or even country, but to a very remarkable extent between confessions obtained in different countries and at different periods.

The point is important because it long constituted a strong argument in favour of the reality of Witchcraft, although unbiased analysis quickly reveals the reasons for this similarity.

The first reason is to be found in the fact that the confessions were obtained almost without exception by means of leading questions of which they were but the echo. The victim was made to confess under torture; death was unavoidable either way, and the object was to attain this consummation with the least possible preparatory pain. The rites of the infernal Sabbat being once fixed, visions and consequent confessions assumed a determinate and invariable form, as invariable in fact as the schedule of prepared questions in answer to which the tortured victims had but just the strength to murmur yes or no.

The second reason is to be found in the common origin of these manifestations, and is indeed a strong argument in favour of the thesis we have exposed. We shall show that early festivals of a sexual nature had already provided the canvas; the fundamental rites of the Sabbat are quite similar to those of a number of purely religious sects; the Sabbats were brought into prominence by the peculiar atmosphere of the time.

Had the Devil played a minor part in the Middle Ages, and had the consequent fear and apparent reality of Witchcraft not inevitably brought about the intense persecution which itself irretrievably confirmed the delusion on account of the mass of torture-extracted confessions, it is more than probable that the whole of these manifestations would have been considered merely as heretic cults.

The ceremonial of the Sabbat was not new, neither were Sorcery or crime or sexual disorders; the flowering of this hell-plant in the Middle Ages was due to their combination intensified by the presence of the divinity of evil. Who has not read of the legends of Ionia? The realm of nature was peopled with hordes of ghosts and spirits; mystic lights glowed in the graveyards while legions of livid spectres rose from their graves and stalked abroad in silent gliding horror. Vampires lurked in hidden alcoves waiting till the midnight chimes should call them to the feast of living blood. Lycanthropy was as common then as it ever was in the fifteenth century, and the were-wolf stalked abroad, an object of even greater terror. The incantations of the women of Thesalia in honour of the triple Hecate are legendary.

Considered in the light of reason, bereft of exaggeration and fear-begotten realities, the Sabbat becomes a perverted sexual and criminal cult, and certainly restricted to comparatively few adepts. The enormous number of witches in the Middle Ages was a direct consequence of the laws and form of trial, and one can safely assert that not more than perhaps ten per cent of the victims had any connection with the cult at all.

I now propose to give a description of a typical Sabbat, reconstructed from a large number of similar confessions contained in the Justiciary Records and elsewhere, so that the reader may get a clear and, I hope, vivid impression of its form and characteristic features.

Night has spread a veil of mystery and dread over the countryside; peasant and citizen have hurried along the darkening paths in the gathering twilight, have barred their doors and crept fearfully to bed. The last lingering echos of curfew have long since died away and the world is still. For those that peep from shuttered windows dark shapes move in every shadow, and the night bird's eerie cry sends them shivering away. The moonlight conjures up weird phantasmas as the clouds chase across the sky, and the mists swirl strangely over the marshes where glows the will-o'-the-wisp. To-night all evil is abroad, its power reigns supreme over a world of fear and terror, and unholy creatures gather at the cross-roads where lies the suicide in his lonely grave; the tombs give up their dead, the vampire is lurking in the shadows ready to drain the life blood from the unwary, dark elementals are materialising from the aura of the victims' blood, and in the graveyards monstrous hags clasp in gloating frenzy the icy corpses of young men, or smother the death cries of the little children they have lured away. Upon the hillside a sombre dwelling stands. Faint lights shine through the cracks of its closely shuttered windows, and borne upon the night wind a sound of mournful chanting sends the belated traveller hurrying upon his way. A horrible decrepit hag crouches over the seething cauldron within the house, and the flickering light from three tapers of human grease sends fantastic shadows playing grotesquely over the surrounding walls, revealing the white nakedness of two younger women as they stand in awe, but eyes ablaze and limbs aquiver with sexual expectancy.

Around the triangle formed by the three tapers a strip of human skin is nailed upon the ground, and on this circle lie a black cat's head, a bat, a ram's horns, and a human skull, while in the centre is drawn the inverted or infernal pentacle. Strange herbs are smouldering on neighbouring tripods, and dense acrid smoke swirls in thick clouds about the room. Higher and higher rises the moaning chant, the smouldering fires burst into flame and die away, the spell is complete. From a black jar, the hag extracts an evil-smelling ointment and, chanting still, anoints her two companions with it. And now they stand before the empty hearth, burning with incipient drug-begotten madness, and between their thighs they hold hard-pressed long poles rudely carved to Phallic semblance or brooms of legendary fame. They are away; as some hell blast blows screaming up the chimney they are whisked out into the night, up overhead into the chasing clouds where other frenzied shadowy forms sweep onwards to the ghastly moor.

And slowly, from its lonely stillness where the great stones of forgotten worships rear their strange darker outlines against the scurrying clouds, or where some ruined chapel spreads its mutilated ivy-covered arches, the moor becomes alive with silent movement. Fantastic riders swoop down from the surrounding darkness, weird beings half animal, half human, crawl in awful stealth from the shadows, men and women gather here and there in groups. Great fires blaze forth, and a vast assembly scatters its increasing numbers over the surrounding ground. Strange lights hover in the trees near by, and dark bats flit overhead in ever-narrowing circles. The wind sweeps over the country in shrieking gusts, and the stench of corruption rises from the offerings. Around the cauldrons the witches are brewing poisonous mixtures, toads and vipers, corpse flesh, children's limbs, fresh blood, are brewed with deadly drugs. Here crimes are planned, deadly poisons pass from hand to hand. Let enemies beware. To-morrow some lingering sickness will decimate their flock, or drive them slowly to the grave. Children also attend the Sabbat, and by the pond, the dark waters of which gleam in the fitful moonlight, they watch over and herd the flock of toads and reptiles. A sudden silence falls over the motley crowd, the wind breaks forth in one great tempestuous blast, and the Presence appears. Enthroned in the centre of the moor he sits dark and forbidding, his horns curl upward in awful majesty, and between them burns a fiery flame. His dark wings are spread behind him, and his body is covered with opalescent scales. One by one his subjects approach and hail him, kissing him *in anno*. And as they do so their spells and poisons are consecrated by the Prince of Evil.

To him is brought the fairest maiden that she may be queen of the Sabbat, and on the altar-stone before his throne she writhes in a voluptuous agony of pain under the all-rending action of his monstrous sex. And now on all sides weird music and discordant chanting arise, the feast has begun, corrupt flesh is greedily devoured, aphrodisiac drugs are absorbed, and madness spreads through the crowd. Faster and more furiously do they dance and stamp, couples sway to the sexual rhythm, hag and youth, maiden and beast, incubi, succubi, devil and human, till the night rings with the frenzied cries of their unbridled passion.

The more monstrous the perversion, the more hybrid the couple, the greater the merit, till the first delicate shades of approaching dawn send the hell-brood scurrying into the darkness whence they came.

Such was the Sabbat of the Middle Ages. Which of the facts contained in these accounts can we consider as real or objective, and which can we admit to be visionary or subjective 5?

That gatherings for the purpose of sexual worship did actually take place we cannot doubt; there is ample proof to be found of the existence and frequency of such assemblies. They were, as we have pointed out, little different from the recognised meetings of certain religious sects. The devotees of these rites were drugged and maddened and their sexual excesses were normal manifestations of those particular cults. But the attendance of such gatherings would seem to have been restricted and confined to the very few, a relatively very small proportion of so-called witches. By far the greater number never left their beds, where, once anointed with the requisite drugs, they would he in a stupor, while through their minds passed the extravagant visions born of overwrought imaginations, which culminated in intense sexual orgasms. I have before me the recipe of one of the ointments in question, though for obvious reasons I cannot give here its composition, and the peculiar nature of the mixture leaves little doubt as to the results of its application. It is in short a mixture in cunning proportions of sleep-producing drugs and powerful aphrodisiacs. The older witches were tormented by restrained and unsatisfied desires, and jealous of life and love; the source of their burning desires anointed with the drug, they fell into sleep, a prey to frenzied dreams and visions which had that particular character of reality which certain drugs are known to produce. These women, and the all-pervading Devil-Myth gave the sexual cult of the Middle Ages its particular characteristic atmosphere, and the rich lore of Sorcery and consequent criminality added to its wealth of horrors.

If we carefully examine the Sabbat, separate the real from the unreal, we can trace the cult thus defined to its true origins.

The Sabbat from what we have seen consisted essentially of a gathering or assembly over which presided the Devil, the main attribute of his worship being sex. Preparations for this assembly consisted in the absorption through the skin or otherwise of aphrodisiacs and stupefying drugs. The presiding deity was an abnormal being, sometimes a ram, and in some earlier cases a huge black tom-cat. The unvarying form of homage was the kiss *in anno*, after which a meal followed which led to a wild sexual orgy as restraint was cast aside and the exasperated passions of the participants given a free hand.

The attendant monsters, the philters and poisons and similar details we may omit as belonging essentially to the realm of Sorcery.

Having thus reduced the apparently complicated rites of the Sabbat to their main unvarying basic forms, to that part of them that was real and objective, we are in a position to compare them with those of a number of purely religious sects.

We have already described the rites of a number of Phallic cults in the chapter devoted to that worship; the following examples are given here because they have a more direct bearing on the Sabbat itself, but they naturally form part of the same category.

The following description is taken from the rites of the Stedingins, a sect akin to the Waldenses, and the date is 1232, that is two hundred years at least before the first appearance of the Sabbats and the persecutions against Witchcraft.

The assemblies of this sect took place in cellars or other secret places, and the main feature of the cult was a banquet at which presided a large toad or black cat. When the banquet was over there appeared a large black cat that was put on the table, and the master, and afterwards all in turn, kissed it under the tail. At the close of the ceremony the lights were put out, and each man taking the first woman that came to hand had sexual intercourse with her. (Baronius, Annales Ecclesiastici, Tome XXI, page 89.) This is, of course, very similar to the rites of the Sabbat, and if we carefully examine the records of the accusations against many other heretic sects, including in particular those directed against the Knights Templars, we find identical ceremonies described. All

of these are at least two centuries prior to the first appearance
of the Sabbats in Italy from which they spread to the South of
France. As examples of earlier ceremonies of similar character
we have already mentioned the Liberalia and the Bacchanalia,
all of which ceremonies were purely religious in nature
and were attended by the Church. The festival of Venus,
and the Floralia if possible, excelled all others as regards
licentiousness. Ausonius, in whose time (the later half of the
fourth century) the Floralia were still in full force, says: –

'*Nec non lascivi Floralia Laeta theatri*
Quae spectare volunt qui voluisse negant.'
                              Ausonii, *Eglog. de Feriis Romanis*,

The loose women of the town and neighbourhood, called
together by the sounding of horns, mixed with the multitude
in perfect nakedness and excited their passions with obscene
motions and language.

The mysteries of Bacchus were celebrated in Rome in
a special temple and in the sacred wood called Simila near
the river Tiber. At first only women were admitted and
the ceremonies were open and public, until a woman of
Campania, named Priscilla Minia, became high priestess of
the Bacchic rites. From that time on the cult became a secret
one and its nature changed considerably. Wine and drugs
were absorbed by both sexes within the dark catacombs of
the temple and every kind of vice and excess encouraged.
In these midnight assemblies crimes were planned, poisons
prepared and secretly exchanged, denunciations decided, and
all manner of plots hatched.

The cult of Venus was still in existence in the town of Rouen in the seventh century; within the town stood a fortified castle, and in its dungeons followers of this cult preserved similar rites and sexual excesses. (*Vita Sancti Romani*, Thesaut.)

The old orthodox writers dwell on the details of these libidinous rites. The doctrine of the community of women which is to be found at an early date amongst the Adamites was revived in the fifteenth century and can be traced up to the seventeenth century. This doctrine and that of promiscuous sexual intercourse was ascribed by the early Christians to several sects, such as the followers of Florian and of Carpocratian, who used to extinguish the lamps in the churches at the end of the evening services and indulge in sexual intercourse indiscriminately. (*Phillastri*, de Haeresibus.) Epiphanius mentions a sect who sacrificed children in their secret rites. The Gnostics were accused of eating human flesh as well as of lasciviousness, and they were also said to have held their women in common. Both the Gnostics and the Manichcans offered up *Semen Viri* as their sacrament.

A most curious custom prevailed in France as late as the seventeenth century and is especially remarkable in that it took place actually within the churches and was officially recognised by the clergy. The priests of a church elected a 'Bishop of Buffoons,' and this grotesque dignitary, accompanied by a numerous suite, occupied the episcopal throne set in the choir of the church. High Mass was then celebrated, and all the clergy were present and sat with blacked faces, wearing hideous or ridiculous masks, or dressed in fantastic costumes. During the celebration dancers and women passed up and down the aisles singing ribald songs. Others, sitting on the altar, played cards and dice, or waved censers before the priests containing old shoe leather instead of incense. After Mass was over the clergy mingled with the crowd and danced and sang within the church; casks were opened, and soon all restraint was cast aside, the girls and women were stripped naked, and scenes of the utmost licentiousness continued far into the night.

These astonishing ceremonies lasted for twelve or fifteen centuries, and were stamped out only with the greatest difficulty. The presence of the Devil alone was wanting to turn them into regular forms of the Sabbat. Finally, as late as 1890, from the account of an eyewitness who attended the 'love-feast ' after a Methodist 'revival' meeting, we find that in a room at the back of the chapel, the gas lights being turned down, men and women indulged freely in promiscuous sexual intercourse.

These examples could be multiplied indefinitely and serve as examples both for the present chapter and for that on Phallic worship proper. It is hardly necessary to point out their significance. They give us conclusive proof that religious cults identical in form with the Sabbat existed continuously from the remotest antiquity to the present times, and that the characteristic Sabbat of the Middle Ages was merely an episode in the history of these Phallic cults, tainted with the prevalent Sorcery and superstition of the times, and presided over by the Prince of Evil.

CHAPTER VIII

INCUBI AND SUCCUBI AND PSEUDO-MORPHIC PHENOMENA

'For the blood is the life.'

I HAVE grouped together in this chapter a series of phenomena which are important on account of the frequency with which they occur and the fact that they are common to most countries and races. They do not properly belong to Sorcery and they cannot be classified under the heading of Black Magic, they are unique in their peculiar nature.

The chapter is really divided into two distinct parts, the first dealing with the Incubus and Succubus, the second with lycanthropy and vampirism, the only feature common to these two groups of phenomena being that they do not fall under any particular heading in the classification I have elsewhere defined.

The existence of the phenomena belonging to both these groups is substantiated by innumerable and astonishingly consistent accounts, and here again we find them identical both in form and detail at very widely different periods in the world's history.

This may not appear to be extraordinary or unexpected as regards the first group, which can be easily explained, but it is considerably stranger as regards the second group, a far more difficult problem, the solutions of which are very far from being satisfactory or convincing.

However much legend and superstition impress quite definite and invariable forms of belief on the minds of the people, yet there must always be some starting point, some foundation on which to build. In the case of lycanthropy and vampirism such an original basis is extremely difficult to find. In spite of this there are few legends or beliefs that have enjoyed such widespread popularity or had such a number of authenticated accounts, such significant details, or such unvarying forms. In the case of the Sabbat, the similarity of accounts and number of confessions was entirely due to the leading questions of the accusation and the inevitable torture, but in the present case we cannot claim this argument. In cases of vampirism, at any rate, there was no question of arrest, persecution, or torture, the vampire was a living-dead corpse and beyond the clutches of human justice. There could be no confessions; we are yet faced with the unvarying accounts of actual witnesses, and the corroborating evidence is at first sight very convincing. Even in cases of lycanthropy, trials for this crime are so rare as to be practically inexistent, and anyway lycanthropy is easier to explain.

The Incubi and Succubi can be rapidly dismissed; beyond any doubt they have their origin in the phenomenon of nocturnal auto-erotism. Unable to find any explanation of this nervous disorder, people endowed it with personality and considered it as a case of actual sexual connection with creatures of another world.

In the Middle Ages, the period of renaissance of these dark legends, these beings were known as Incubi when they were of the male sex and Succubi when they were of the female sex. They were familiar to Egyptian civilisation, and the Greeks and Romans knew them as *Ephialtes* (from εφιαλλω 'I spring on') and *Insultor* (from 'in sulto,' same meaning).

There are, moreover, several legends as old as the world that may have contributed towards the belief in Incubi and Succubi as an explanation for nocturnal autoerotism. One of these we have already mentioned, the legend of Adam and Lilith and the corresponding relations of Eve with Samael, which occurs in various forms in all the older lore and traditions. The other describes how the gods found the daughters of man beautiful and had connection with them, and is mentioned in the book of Enoch.

How real the existence of such beings was held to be and how literally the legend was accepted, may be gathered from the following account which I have taken at random from a numerous collection of similar examples. This account also gives us a very good idea of the way in which the deeply rooted beliefs and superstitions of the time influenced witnesses so as to cause them unconsciously to distort the facts till no semblance of the truth remained. Reading between the lines of the narrative, however, one may see that here at least was no true case of even auto-erotism, and both the very horrible monster and his violent exit point to a distinctly human agency. The story loses much of its piquancy by translation from the old French, but I have tried to reproduce this as faithfully as possible.

'In the district of Marrfe lived a girl who was with child through the wiles of the Devil. It puzzled her parents not a little to account for her state, for she habitually shunned all manner of dancing and would not marry. On pressing her with questions she confessed that the Devil slept with her every night in the shape of a fine young man. The parents, not content with this explanation, made sudden entrance into the chamber where she slept with torches in their hands. They saw in the bed with her a horrible monster quite inhuman in aspect whom, refusing to leave the bed, they fetched a priest to exorcise. Finally the monster was prevailed upon to leave, which he did with frightful noise and breaking of furniture, removing a portion of the roof in his rage. Three days later the girl gave birth to a monster, the ugliest that was ever seen, which the midwives strangled.'

The explanation of this group of phenomena obviously presents no particular difficulties, and we can now transfer our attention to the metamorphic phenomena of lycanthropy and vampirism.

The fundamental difference between these lies in the fact that in the case of lycanthropy the perpetrator is alive and it is his double, and in some cases he himself who stalks abroad in the form of an animal, while in the case of vampirism he is dead and it is the corpse itself or its emanation that causes the phenomena described. But a very close bond or kinship exists between them, they are both cases of pseudo-morphic bilocation, and accounts of instantaneous repercussion on the corpse in the one case and on the living human body in the other, when the form abroad is hit or wounded, are common to both. Lycanthropy, as I have stated, occurs in two different forms. In one the sorcerer is lying asleep in his bed, while his double, the 'astral body' of the Magi, wanders out in search of victims. In the second case the sorcerer transforms himself materially into the form of an animal. This second form is obviously a corruption and superstitious elaboration of the first, which is the earliest found in history, and the secret of the origin of both forms therefore lies in the origin of the former. This may be taken as being threefold; we have seen that cases of bilocation proper were common in narratives of the past, as for instance in the case of Julian Cox. Such bilocation is a common feature of hypnotic manifestations and something akin to it, when we allow for the inevitable exaggerations and credulity of the narrators, exists in the mediumistic phenomena of the present day. It is indeed easier to imagine a sorcerer while in hypnotic trance picturing himself haunting the familiar countryside in the form of a wolf or other animal than to imagine the witch attending in her drug-produced stupor the complicated ceremonial of the Sabbat.

We find a second possible part-origin when we examine the corresponding Nagualism of Mexican lore. The following account of a case of Nagualism is taken from the *Geographical Description of the Province of Santo-Domingo* by the Reverend Jesuit Father Burgoa, chapter LXXI.

Nagualism was a pact, an alliance, offensive and defensive, between a human being and an animal. The Nagual may be a crocodile, a lion, a serpent, a bird, or any form of animal to whom the native is attached from childhood by an indissoluble fluidic bond. For the native the Nagual is an alter-ego, and during the whole of his life he remains in close connection with the animal who befriends and protects him. Examples of Nagualism are very numerous and certified by apparently unimpeachable witnesses.

'While riding by the shore of a lake the reverend Father Diego was attacked by an enormous crocodile. Spurring his horse, he fought the animal with his iron-tipped staff and finally left it for dead by the edge of the water. On returning to the mission house the first person he meets tells him that a young Indian whom he had some days previously chastised has been taken inexplicably ill. The young Indian was suffering from wounds exactly similar to those inflicted on the crocodile and died simultaneously with his Nagual, the remains of which had been fetched in on the first discovery of these remarkable facts.'

Owing to the impossibility of verifying facts of this nature we can hardly draw any conclusions as to the reality or otherwise of the phenomenon in question, but it suggests that one of the part-origins of lycanthropy may have been the power of some individuals to control animals and direct their ferocious instincts to serve their own ends. This, of course, would not explain the phenomenon of repercussion, but apart from the consideration that a badly wounded animal might well turn upon its master there is very little evidence of its existence. The whole question of repercussion is very similar in many respects to certain results brought about by hypnotism and trance and known as exteriorisation. The appearance of wounds on individuals of a certain highly nervous temperament is not unknown, and cases where these wounds correspond to the wounds of

Christ on the cross are quite common. We enter here into the domain of pathology, such cases being due to one of the rarer forms of hysteria.

The last of the three sources to which we may look as the probable origin of lycanthropy is the somewhat rare disease which bears its name. As a pathological state, lycanthropy may be described as a form of hysteria. It is characterised by the patient's belief that he has been metamorphosed into an animal and is accompanied by a craving for strange foods, including the flesh of living beings. The patients are yellow in complexion, have hollow eyes and a dry tongue, and run on all fours laughing or barking hideously.

It does not take much inflation or imagination for the victim of this complaint to become the were-wolf of the legend.

In the case of vampirism, however, no such simple explanations are forthcoming. Some writers have suggested that the accidents caused by large blood-sucking vampire bats were responsible for the legend of vampirism. But I would point out that in the great majority of cases vampirism was rampant in countries such as Transylvania where the vampire bat is and was always totally unknown.

In fact the countries where such bats are found are in most cases free from the belief in vampirism and can in no sense be regarded as the countries from which the legend originated. Indeed the bat derived its name from the human vampire, which seems to be of Serbian origin, 'Wampir.' This belief prevails chiefly in Russia, Poland, and Serbia, amongst the Czechs of Bohemia, and the other Slavonic races of Austria. It was especially prevalent from 1730 to 1735.

The belief was well known, however, to the Greeks and Romans under the name of 'Broucolaques,' and among other forms of early vampirism these creatures were supposed to chew and masticate audibly in their graves, as described in Ranft's *De masticatione mortuorum in tumulis* (1734).

As I have already pointed out, there is a very marked similarity between all accounts of vampirism and this is somewhat difficult to explain. The reader can judge for himself from the examples quoted hereafter, each of which is chosen in order to bring out some special point to which I shall call attention after each narrative. We will first consider the general form or outline common to all those narratives when once they are bereft of exaggeration and the circumstances peculiar to each case.

Some man in a community dies. Usually he leaves a will containing strange instructions about the disposal of his body, but this is by no means a general rule. It is soon noticed that a number of people are suffering from anaemia and loss of blood and deaths occur which seem unaccountable. Witnesses declare they have seen strange shapes moving in the night and following solitary human beings. The corpse is exhumed and found, though cold and immobile, to be free from any signs of corruption or rigor mortis. The lips are red, the eyes are open, and the hair and nails have grown. According to the traditional rites a stake was driven through the creature's heart, the head was separated from the trunk, and the mouth filled with garlic.

The first example is taken from the *Magia Posthuma* of Charles Ferdinand de Schertz (Olmutz, 1706). A shepherd from the village of Blw, near the town of Kadam in Bohemia, was suspected after his death of being the cause of the slow loss of vitality and death of a number of people. On exhuming his body it was found to be quite free from corruption, and although attempts were made to drive a stake through the body (apparently unsuccessfully), he was again seen abroad on the following night. After a second exhumation the body was handed over to the executioner and conveyed in a cart from the village to a field in order that it might be burnt. The corpse howled and struggled, kicking and moving its legs and arms as though alive, and on a new stake being driven through its body, screamed and bled profusely. The corpse was then burnt to ashes and the victims recovered.

The curious point about this narration is that the vampire was actually seen to move and cry out in daylight by several people, contrarily to the majority of cases, where the corpse itself lies absolutely still. The case for this reason strongly suggests suspended animation. Vampirism at one time became so frequent in Hungary that the custom arose of differing burial in all cases, and if any evidence of suspended corruption was observed the body was burnt.

The next episode is duly authenticated and witnessed, and is extracted from the *Lettres Juives*, 1738 edition, letter 137. The narrative is attested by two officers of the tribunal of Belgradia and by an officer of the guards stationed at Gradfich, all of whom were ocular witnesses of the facts related.

In the early part of September an inhabitant of the village of Kisilova, three miles out of the village of Gradfich, died, being sixty-two years of age. Three days after being buried he appeared to his son during the night and asked him for food. After getting this he vanished. The next day the son spread his extraordinary news about the village. That night his father did not reappear. But after the following night the son was found dead in his bed.

On the same day five or six people in the village sickened mysteriously and died one after another within the week. The bailiff sent an account of these events to the Tribunal of Belgradia and two officers and the executioner were sent down to investigate. All the graves of those who had died during the last six weeks were opened and the corpses examined, but on coming to that of the old man he was found with eyes wide open and blood-red lips, no sign of corruption could be detected, and he was considered to be a vampire. None of the other corpses showed any similar symptoms. This event occurred in 1732.

The interesting point about this narrative is that instead of going direct to the grave of the suspected man, all the graves of those who had recently died were examined, and it was in his case only that the symptoms were observed, which coincided with the facts divulged by the man's son only two days after the burial, when no signs of vampirism had as yet appeared.

The next case tells of a man called Arnold Paul, an inhabitant of Medreiga (1729-1730). It is similar in every way, so that a description would be mere repetition, but its singular interest lies in the fact that the man was killed originally by being horribly crushed between two carts, which would seem definitely to exclude any possibility of catalepsy or suspended animation.

Keeping these examples before our minds, let us try to reason out what explanation can be given that will meet the facts.

It would appear necessary to assume the simultaneous existence either of suspended animation or perhaps of some particular conditions preserving the corpses from corruption, and of some kind of epidemic of a disease similar to anaemia or possibly sleeping sickness. That certain grounds and atmospheres have a marked preserving effect on corpses is well known. At Toulouse in France is a crypt below a monastery where corpses remain absolutely untouched by any incipient corruption, some of which have been there over two centuries. They are lined up against the wall and seem almost alive. Yet, in a neighbouring cellar, separated from the former only by a wall, these conditions do not exist. An exactly similar crypt exists under the famous monastery at Kiev in Southern Russia. I have personally visited both these places and can vouch for the accuracy of the facts.

The only possible conclusion we can draw from an examination of the facts connected with vampirism is that in those places where it prevailed there existed certain graves and vaults which possessed the preserving quality, although neighbouring graves might not, and that occasional outbreaks of some epidemic, coupled through superstition with the above fact, gave rise to the legend which was to people the night with further terrors.

The fact that vampirism was in a very great number of cases apparently hereditary adds considerable force to this argument, since the members of one family being buried in one particular vault the possibility of the corpses being kept free from corruption is much increased.

Of course, suspended animation while in a state of catalepsy, self-produced or otherwise, is quite common among the Fakirs of the East, for example. These cases are too well known to bear further repetition, but Fakirs have been known to remain buried in the ground for six months and more without any apparent damage to their health. Such cases as these have been witnessed when extremely elaborate precautions had been taken to ensure the absence of fraud, and in fact fraud seems entirely out of the question under the conditions described.

Bearing these remarks in mind, we must leave the reader to conclude as he may wish. The case of vampirism is mysterious, and while one obviously cannot accept the idea of the objective existence of such beings, a really convincing explanation that will meet all the facts is not easily found.

There is, however, another possible explanation, but in the present state of our knowledge of these matters it would be quite premature were I to give it more than a passing mention. It is a bare possibility, an unknown factor, no more, and it is itself so mysterious, if it should prove to be true, that it is more in the nature of a further deepening of the mystery than an elucidation.

We shall see in the chapter dealing with Magic Initiation how considerable was the part played by what we have there termed elementals. They are beings that are not of this world as we understand it, indeed there is no reason whatever to substantiate the belief that they exist at all. They constitute at the most a very vague working theory when some explanation of the mysteries connected with modern metapsychics is sought for, and until the untiring efforts of scrupulous investigators have brought more substantial and demonstrated facts to light from the chaos of spiritualism and mediumistic phenomena, nothing can be said about this strange theory one way or the other. I have attempted to give some hint as to their possible nature in the chapter I mention, but we are here within the realm of pure unfounded speculation.

If, however, we are willing to admit for a single instant the possible existence of such beings, then we can suggest another explanation for vampirism. It is this explanation that is given in the writings of initiates who of course believed in elemental and claimed control over them. It was their belief that such creatures being immaterial, it is necessary in order that they may act in the material plane to afford them the possibility of materialisation. The methods by means of which this end can be achieved are given in the rituals of Magic. Now, such elemental beings were endowed with the power of entering a human body recently vacated by the 'soul' of its previous owner, or temporarily vacated in cases of catalepsy or mediumistic trance, and in this way the writers of these works explain both the phenomena of vampirism and those akin to modern mediumistic manifestations. Naturally the elemental would seek some way of feeding its material body, and we must also bear in mind that elementals were always considered to be intensely inimical to mankind, and the most solemn warnings are given in the rituals lest the unwary should call them into being and fail to control them. A chapter on vampirism, like the chapter on Magic proper, would not be complete without a passing mention of this theory, and, as I have said, some writers of the present day have a strong leaning towards it as the only acceptable working theory that will meet the singular facts of modern metapsychics.

However that may be, I personally incline to the theory I have already given of a coincidence of corpse-preserving vaults and some recurring epidemic unknown to early medicine, coupled with the strong all-pervading influence of superstition.

The matter is one for speculation, and in the absence of further facts no conclusion is possible.

CHAPTER IX

DIVINATION AND ASTROLOGY

'Astra influunt, non cogunt.'

Picus de la Mirandola.

The various practices grouped under the denomination of divination together form one of the most important chapters in the history of the occult, although it is only possible to give a brief outline of their main characteristics within the scope of these essays. Divination included a very great number of different practices, the common object of which was the acquirement of knowledge concerning future events. Whereas the various forms of the occult which we have already dealt with, such as Sorcery, Black Magic, Satanism, and the Sabbat, were evil in tendency and had earned universal reprobation, when we examine divination we find an altogether different state of things. Divination was considered as an art and a science, a part of statecraft, and no important expedition was started, no decision arrived at, no step taken until some favourable indication had been obtained by means of divination. Moreover, whereas an examination of Sorcery or Black Magic has led us to the conclusion that there was no foundation for the belief in any mysterious powers connected with these practices beyond the potentialities of actual criminal actions, the same cannot be said of some forms of divination.

For the first time we come across evidence of the existence of a definite gift or power, hyperesthesis, or better, cryptesthesis, phenomena known as monitions and premonitions, and distinct forms of clairvoyance, sometimes mediumistic, more generally auto-hypnotic. We find the first definite link between the occult science of the past and modem metapsychics, and cryptesthesis as defined by Richet, was undoubtedly known to antiquity and brought into divination that element of truth which so strongly contributed towards its universal popularity.

When we come to examine the various forms of divination we will find that the greater number of these were due to the unconscious muscular control of apparently uncontrolled movements (divining pendulum, etc.), or to chance alone, but some of these practices resulted in clear cases of auto-hypnotic trance and consequent cryptesthesis, and these are of course by far the most interesting.

Divination and Initiatic Magic are, in a sense, closely related to one another. Although they are very different, both in aim and form, certain processes of divination were used by the initiates while certain ceremonies and invocations that belong more properly to the ritual of Magic were used in divination. Necromancy, for example, is purely magical as regards its ceremonial and rites, but belongs to divination as regards object and aim.

It is often taken for granted that divination is concerned exclusively with the future. This is not strictly true; divination and all rites and practices connected with it included careful study of past and present, and in most cases divination could be more accurately defined as the interpretation of past and present events considered as clues from which prognostics can be drawn.

The principle underlying divination, the idea that the gods and spirits not only conduct human affairs but are moreover willing to give signs or warnings of their intentions for the especial benefit of man, is a very remarkable one indeed. The belief that from the manner of occurrence or form of one or several events the form of future events can be logically deduced, is a simpler and older conception of the same principle, and so long as there is some relationship between the facts examined and the facts predicted the system is logical enough. An examination of the heavens, winds, and clouds, for instance, as a means of predicting a favourable or unfavourable sea voyage is a logical deduction from related facts, whereas the examination of the entrails of a hen to determine the suitability or otherwise of a military expedition requires the theory of divine intervention for explanation.

The belief in the possibility of learning the intentions of the gods is a direct consequence of the original animistic systems in the same way as the belief in the possibility of influencing natural phenomena by means of prayer, propitiation, or conjuration.

Divination was both universal and extremely powerful, it formed part of statecraft, was taught by old-established and venerable schools, praised by the poets, demonstrated by philosophers and accepted and practised by all. Divination cannot be considered merely as a branch of the occult, its importance is far greater, and whatever may have been the part apportioned to credulity, to fraud, to true cryptesthesis, to chance pure and simple, or to the more probable fact that astute statesmen relied on this method to convince both ruler and nation of the advisability of adopting their views, and to relieve themselves of heavy responsibilities in the event of failure, we must consider divination as one of the most important influences in the history of the world.

In all countries where divination was practised on a large scale, such as Greece, for instance, great pride was taken in the fact by the nation as a whole. Rich presents and splendid offerings were brought to Greece when foreign princes landed on her shores, attracted from afar by the fame of her oracles. Moreover, the belief in the reality of divination strengthened the belief in the gods which might well otherwise have waned and disappeared among the highly civilised populations of both Greece and Rome. Divination in Greece and Rome, in Egypt and the East, proved to be the mainstay of the later religious systems, the most important occupation of the priesthood, and gave them that supreme control over the decisions of the kings and councils which it had always been their ambition to hold.

Clearly, the decisions of augurs and oracles must have been fairly satisfactory on the whole. How else can we account for the quite extraordinary favour acquired and maintained by divination?' The priesthood were, of course, directly concerned in the success or otherwise of the oracles, but the rulers and leaders, unless they happened to be themselves members of the school of augury, would hardly appreciate the existence of a power greater than theirs, a sort of supreme court whose ruling on any matter was practically final, and whose sanction they were bound to seek in matters of even comparatively minor importance. We can only conclude that antiquity found the pronouncements of its various oracles entirely satisfactory, but this does not imply that their science was a true one, or that they were actually able to foretell events. However little or however much they may have been due to actual cryptesthesis, the cryptic answers of both oracles and augurs, the complex rules of their art, allowing great freedom of interpretation, the prudence which characterised their pronouncements, all point to wise and astute statesmanship within the state, and we can only give those men our unreserved admiration for the way in which they handled the powerful tool which controlled the destinies of men and nations.

The greater part of the superstitions that have survived and to this day influence the thoughts of men are connected directly or indirectly with divination, or more exactly with one branch of divination, the belief in omens.

Few individuals, however civilised and educated they may be, are entirely free from some form of superstition. In most cases it is only a matter of impressions, impressions of impending evil, premonitions of misfortune or of success, events in our lives become associated with minor incidents the recurrence of which recalls vividly before our minds the happy or unhappy occurrence. We find ourselves establishing a distinct connection between the one and the other; gradually we come to regard apparently trivial incidents as presages of good or evil, especially if some fortuitous coincidence has justified our half-formed belief. One positive case will stand out where a hundred negative results have remained unheeded, and certain animals, certain tunes, certain places, certain people, certain objects will be everlastingly associated in our minds with fortune or misfortune; some have become omens, others charms. We have subconsciously developed a belief in divination and a form of Magic; we call it superstition. How many men or women can sincerely state that they are entirely free from any such belief?

The idea of presage or omens, signs, and indications as to the nature of coming events is an idea that occurs naturally to the human mind. In some senses it is a correct idea, and when we turn to metapsychics we shall see that monitions, and what is stranger still, premonitions, are not only quite frequent but undeniably real. If this idea of divination or belief in omens creeps into the minds of men in this age of materialism and relative atheism we can easily understand its predominance in the polytheistic eras of the past, when trees and glades, brooks and hills, storms, winds and seasons had each a divinity, demons and spirits, and the night and the day were peopled with a host of supernatural beings.

Divination is in fact the earliest form of a religious science and ceremonies and methods for interrogating the gods are to be found in the earliest records of Chaldea, amongst the religious practices of every sect or system in the world, and amongst the practices of natives and savages in the darkest corners of the earth. Man is constantly preoccupied about his future, his life, about the outcome of his love affairs or his financial occupations, and when we consider the horde of fortune-tellers, crystal-gazers, cartomancers, chiromancers and others who have thrived on the world's credulity from the remotest antiquity to the present day, we can understand the reasons for which divination was popular, universal and powerful. The soothsayers of Bond Street are not so far removed from their Theban predecessors, and they are consulted quite as often, and undoubtedly on the same subjects.

The oldest traditions connected with fortune-telling have depended on this practice as a means of living for countless generations. Although the gypsy uses many methods of divination, and, incidentally, some forms of Sorcery, the one great traditional method is that of the Taro cards which we have already mentioned. Although the method is governed by strict rules the operator is given great latitude as regards interpretation; moreover the gypsy is a good physiognomist and quite often gifted with cryptesthesic powers which various factors account for his success.

We will now define divination, its various forms or subdivisions, and examine and describe each in turn.

Divination is a very complex art and consists of a number of different practices entirely distinct from one another. A general division or classification gives us the following headings.

Divination can first be divided into two main branches:

(*a*)   Autoscopic phenomena.
(*b*)   Heteroscopic phenomena.

By autoscopic divination we mean such methods as depend entirely on the conscious or subconscious personality of the soothsayer, and this branch can be subdivided again into Sensory Automatism, Motor Automatism, and Mental Impressions.

Crystal-gazing, a very widespread method of divination, is an example of sensory automatism, and shell-hearing is a somewhat less familiar form of the same phenomenon.

The divining rod is one of the best-known examples of motor automatism, of which other examples are the pendulum or suspended ring, which is common to many countries, water divining, coscinomancy, or divining by means of a sieve, the ordeal by Bible and key of the Middle Ages, and the ordeal by fire. Divination by means of automatic writing is very common in China but belongs to the more cultured classes.

Trance speaking and auto-hypnotic phenomena come under this heading. Dreams and their interpretation are examples of mental impressions.

The second main division, heteroscopic divination, is based on the examination of events or facts entirely beyond the control of the operator. This large division comprises a number of varied practices, the most important of which are:–

Sortilege, or the casting of lots or dice; the astragali or knucklebones were intended for this purpose.
Haruspication, or the inspection of the entrails of animals.
Scapulomancy, or divination by means of the spealbone.
Augury and Omens.
Astrology.

The second branch, or heteroscopic aspect of divination, is the most varied and the most complex, but it is by far the least interesting of the two. A cursory examination of the various rites connected with it will suffice to show that it is merely a curious mixture of Sympathetic Magic and symbolism, association of ideas and analogy, together with a certain amount of scientific observation.

The first branch or autoscopic part of divination is of quite remarkable interest, and we will examine it with some care and compare it with the results obtained by modern investigators under the name of cryptesthesis.

It is among the practices of this first class of divinatory formulae that a real gift or power is to be found, whereas the heteroscopic phenomena may be classed as a varied collection of superstitions, belief in which was only possible on account of the success and relative reality of the autoscopic methods.

The true interest of divination therefore lies in autoscopic practices, but before we examine these we will briefly describe the more important types of heteroscopic formulae.

Heteroscopic divination, or the art of deducing events from occurrences unrelated to them, from the behaviour of animals, the inspection of entrails, and other means, is the oldest form of Mantic science. It seems to have existed from the earliest origins in all countries, and to have persisted in one form or another almost to the present day. Its flourishing period was in the earliest times, and as soon as autoscopic practices were introduced and began to spread, mantic heteroscopy faded into the background, and although it was ever present, it was confined to popular and private use, whereas autoscopic divination took its former place and ruled rulers and nations.

Mantic deductive systems or heteroscopy are primarily the natural result of animistic theurgies; they are also a direct consequence of the symbolic and homoeopathic tendencies of early civilisations . We have laid great stress on the importance of symbolism, and on the universal habit of symbolical expression which prevailed in the earlier periods of history, and which is still a characteristic feature of the mental processes of Eastern nations. This great tendency to express their ideas, doctrines, beliefs by means of symbols, their thoughts by the use of parable and story, together with the presence of an animistic cosmos, provides the necessary material for the elaboration of just such a system as heteroscopy.

The deductions were at first quite simple, and the symbolism direct and straightforward. Omithomancy, for instance, must have arisen from such simple observations as the rise and fall of an eagle or vulture at a given time as indicating the success or failure of a proposed measure. Such methods as these were used under various forms until more information was required than the mere approbation or condemnation of the proposal, and gradually a whole elaborate system was evolved in which the actions, movements, and behaviour generally of birds or animals, the appearance of certain objects, were given definite meanings, while combinations and sequences of these actions or observations gave the expert soothsayer infinite scope for interpretation.

Every natural occurrence, every incident, was taken into account and its meaning extracted, and natural phenomena were considered to be the language of the gods, the symbolical expression of their thoughts, riddles from which the wise might infer their intentions and so conform the actions of the people to suit the desires of the gods and so ensure success. This was the true aim of divination, and not merely the prediction of an unavoidable succession of events.

The early civilisations were not fatalistic, they used divination, not in order that they might know beforehand what was unavoidably going to pass, but in order to shape their own course according to the indications received so that they might avoid disaster and misfortune and remain successful and prosperous.

Two distinct classes of phenomena were used for heteroscopic divination. Abnormal phenomena, such as storms of unusual violence, the appearance of meteors, eclipses, earthquakes, the abnormal growth of trees or plants, and generally the occurrence of anything outside the normal course of natural laws, on the one hand, and on the other hand, normal phenomena or natural occurrences which through analogy or coincidence, or tradition, were given an artificial meaning. Greater importance was attached to the observation of natural or normal phenomena than to the indications given by abnormal events. The former were subject to definite conventional rules, by means of which their meaning could be read; the latter were, unless previously observed, beyond the knowledge and experience of the soothsayer. Their meaning was vague and difficult to determine, tradition was silent, and the responsibility heavy, for such phenomena could not be allowed to pass unheeded owing to their very nature and the impossibility of keeping them secret. The soothsayer was therefore mainly concerned with the observation of normal natural events.

One of the early forms of heteroscopic divination is ornithomancy, or divination based on the observation of the behaviour of birds. The strongest, largest birds, those whom a solitary life had endowed with a greater individuality, such as birds of prey, were chosen in preference to the other kinds for this purpose. The movements of birds in flight, the direction of their flight, their tendency to rise or fall, were all signs or omens with definite and invariable meanings. Another method of divination was based on their cries and the twittering of the smaller birds, more particularly at dawn or nightfall. In Greek mythology birds and gods were very closely related, a bird being attributed to each deity, the eagle to Zeus, the crow to Apollo, etc.

Alectryomancy, or divination by means of the cock, was a very important branch of ornithomancy both in Greece and Rome. Although many other animals, such as reptiles, locusts, lizards, bees, mice, etc,, were used, ornithomancy seems to have been by far the most popular and most important form of that heteroscopic divination that was based on the observation of animals.

The next important division of heteroscopy is Haruspication, or divination by means of the examination of the entrails of animals. Haruspication and ornithomancy were by far the most important forms of heteroscopic divination, and as we are mainly concerned in these essays with autoscopic divination, we will confine ourselves to the examination of these two main forms as typical of the art as a whole.

Haruspication most probably arose from the earlier practice of inferring from the position or attitude of animals at the moment of, and just after, sacrifice, whether the offering was acceptable to the gods. The liver was the part of the entrails most frequently chosen for inspection, and it was believed that in order that traces should be found of divine influence the liver must be that of an animal entirely free from passion, an apathetic and pacific animal, such as the lamb, for instance. Such animals as the cock were unfit for haruspication as being subject to desire, anger, and pride. The liver was examined with regard to colour, size, and shape; the existence or absence of marks was noted, and the position of the organ within the body and its healthy or unhealthy state. It was then usually blunt or boiled, and again examined and more indications derived from the circumstances attending these manipulations.

Autoscopy consists of sensory and motor automatism, trance utterance, crystal gazing, and the perception of monitions and premonitions. Here we are more interested in methods than in the historical aspect of the question. All the methods used by autoscopic soothsayers of antiquity persist at the present day, and have been taken up and closely examined by scientists, the particular phenomenon on which its various forms are based being known as Cryptesthesis, one of the main branches of experimental metapsychics.

Sensory automatism, or trance utterance, is represented in the past by the Sibyls and the Oracles. These are the two outstanding features of this branch of autoscopy.

The sibyls belonged to a system of individual prophecy, whereas the oracles were collective institutions, they were otherwise very similar, and the various forms of oracles only differed from one another through the methods employed.

But the true nature of the Greek sibyls is not to be found in their prophetic gifts, but in the unreality and immaterial side of their being which places them in a class apart, akin to that of nymphs. They are perhaps incomplete divinities, the hybrid and belated product of Greek imagination, ideas which it was now too weak to endow with permanent and concrete personality.

The truly interesting feature of autoscopic divination is to be found in an examination of the divining methods used in the oracles of Greece. These oracles were attached to definite places, and differ from ordinary methods of divination in that they were organised and maintained by a brotherhood of priests.

A cavern, a spring, or a wood was endowed by popular fancy with supernatural qualities. From being used as a favourite spot where the usual forms of heteroscopic divination might be practised with advantage, it would gradually be brought under the control of an organised priesthood, rites and ceremonies would be instituted, perhaps a temple would be built, and thus a new oracle created. There was a great number of these oracles in Greece, and various forms of divination were used, although by far the greater number used the trance method.

An oracle can best be defined as a special place wherein a deity is supposed to give an answer through the medium of an inspired priest or priestess to the inquiries of its devotees. The most salient example of the trance method employed in oracular divination is afforded by the oracle of Delphis.

During the all-important historical period of this famous oracle, and perhaps from its earnest origins, a woman known as the Pythoness was the organ of inspiration, and it was generally believed that she delivered her oracles under the direct dictation of the god. The divine possession worked like an epileptic seizure, and was exhausting and sometimes dangerous, nor is there any reason to suppose that it was simulated. She began by chewing the leaves of the sacred laurel, and then drank water from the prophetic stream called Kassotis; but the culminating point was reached when she seated herself upon the tripod. And here, according to the belief of at least the later ages, she was supposed to be inspired by a mystic vapour that arose from a fissure in the ground.

Against the ordinary explanation of this as a real mephitic gas producing convulsions there seem to be geological and chemical objections, nor have the recent excavations revealed any chasm or gap in the floor of the temple.

The Pythoness was no ambitious pretender but ordinarily a virtuous woman of the lower classes. It is probable that what she uttered were only unintelligible murmurs, and that these were interpreted into relevance and set in metric or prose sentences by the 'holy ones,' or members of the leading Delphic families who sat around the tripod and received the questions of the consultant beforehand.

That these answers were prepared in advance or altered and modified to suit the question or the wish of the members of the circle is undeniable. But we are nevertheless in presence of cases of trance utterance, of auto-hypnotism, of mediumistic practices in short, which were very similar to those of the present day.

Such trances were often confused with possessions in the Middle Ages, and with the numerous fits and nervous disorders that must have appeared highly mysterious to normal men. Madness, and nervous fits, such as epilepsy and accidental cataleptic trance, were always considered with awe and respect in early days, and later, when Sorcery and Black Magic had already poisoned the minds of men, with terror and loathing. Almost worshipped at first, cruelly persecuted in later times, these abnormal beings became famous soothsayers or initiates, or else perished miserably at the stake. They were sensitive, unbalanced beings, and quite similar to those individuals who are to be found at the present day, and yield so easily to hypnotic influence, or become mediums.

The prophetic gift, or sensorial automatism, the unconscious inspired utterance of sentences, is a fairly common phenomenon, and modem science has shed a new light on the subject, as we shall see in a subsequent chapter.

A very great number of people possess the gift of cryptesthesis to some extent; some are merely sensitive, others are amenable to auto-hypnotic methods; others, again, are apparently controlled by some mysterious influence which seems to invade their brain when in a state of trance. Experiments have proved that we possess within ourselves a power, as yet mysterious and undeveloped, by means of which we may become aware of facts which our normal senses are unable to reveal to us.

This is precisely what the adepts of divination claimed; and, although we can reject all heteroscopic practices as mere superstitious and illogical processes, we are bound to retain autoscopic practices as partly sound from a scientific point of view. We will deal with cryptesthesis in a subsequent chapter.

However strange it may appear, however mysterious may be the power, however difficult it may be for us to control it, to discover its mechanism or to develop it where it exists in rudimentary form, the fact of its reality remains.

There remains only the question of motor automatism, or unconscious muscular action to be examined, and here we are faced with some very interesting problems.

A great variety of methods were employed in connection with this branch of divination, the oldest and most common of which is the divining pendulum. The planchette superseded the pendulum in more recent times, but its principle and the explanation of its mechanism are the same. A weight or ring suspended from a silk thread is held by the operator so that it hangs just over the centre of a circle around which are inscribed the letters of the alphabet. The operator then thinks of a question and remains holding his hand quite still until, after a short time, the pendulum begins to swing, slightly at first, and with increasing amplitude, travelling over one of the letters which is noted. The process is repeated until a message has been obtained. In the case of the planchette, which is a heart-shaped board carrying two small castors at its wide end, and a pencil placed vertically through a hole in its apex, the operator places his hands lightly on the apparatus, which will then move, apparently of its own accord, and write out messages.

Quite obviously fraud is perfectly simple in both cases, and this fact should be constantly borne in mind. Nevertheless, although fraud is practically always present, it is very far from being always intentional or conscious. The operator may be absolutely sincere in his conviction that he has in no way interfered with the free movements of the pendulum or planchette, although he may have constantly exercised the greatest care in order not to communicate any impulse to the instrument, yet, in the great majority of cases, the sole cause of the movement is to be attributed to muscular action on his part, and he is the unconscious writer of the messages obtained. There is, of course, the chance that a word may be spelt out that will have a direct bearing on the point at issue, and the probability is not nearly so small as one might imagine at first sight.

It should be remembered that an infinitesimal impulse, if it is repeated at regular intervals, is sufficient to set the heaviest pendulum in motion, and the planchette, owing to its construction, moves at the slightest touch. A belief in the efficacy of these methods could only be justified on the assumption that in the hands of an operator gifted with cryptesthesic power, this form of subconscious action might enable him to make use of it, whereas he would in the ordinary course of events be unaware of its existence (as is very frequently the case).

There is another form of divination by motor automatism which is derived directly from the pendulum, that is the divining rod.

Experiments conducted with a view to establishing the possibility of discovering buried metals and water by means of the divining rod have led to very curious results, and a chapter on divination would not be complete without a reference to these.

The problem of the divining rod is a very strange one. The facts connected with it belong to the domain of cryptesthesis, or more exactly to that of pragmatic cryptesthesis, that is a cryptesthesis induced in a sensitive subject by the contact or near presence of a material object. A subject under hypnotic influence, a medium, or a specially gifted individual, for instance, will describe a person he has never seen on being given an object belonging to and intimately connected with that person.

The phenomenon can be described as follows:

If a rod of hazel wood of special shape is held in the hands of certain sensitive people in such a way that no strain is put upon it by the operator, under certain conditions the rod twists or bends apparently of its own accord and with considerable force, the movement being entirely independent of the will or actions of the operator.

When the operator, holding the rod in his hands, walks through some part of the country where it is known that there are streams of water flowing under the ground, or buried masses of metal, the rod bends or twists so forcibly that the operator cannot restrain it. Such are the facts. Moreover, they are true. Recent careful experiments have proved this.

The material from which the rod is cut is an important factor. During a series of tests carried out at Toulouse by Paul Lemoine rods made of wood, copper, iron, and glass were used.

Out of eight tests, the wooden rod gave eight correct indications, the copper rod four out of seven, the iron rod two out of four, and the glass rod none. During the same tests A. Vire, D.Sc., was able to trace the course of a subterranean stream for four miles with the greatest accuracy. A considerable number of experiments, which are particularly interesting owing to the care shown by the investigators and the elaborate precautions taken, were conducted a few years ago by MM. Pelaprat, Colonel Vallantin, Probst, the Abbe Mermet, Joulfreau, and A. Vire. The following table gives the result of these experiments:–

	No. of Tests	Percentage of accurate results
Water	19	89
Caverns	23	87
Metals	11	80
Coal	9	55

MM. Pelaprat and Vire on one occasion found indications that water would be discovered in a certain estate, and gave the exact spot where the well should be bored, and the depth at which the water would be found (30 feet), both of which pieces of information were found to be absolutely accurate, although on several previous occasions the owner had sunk wells in the near vicinity in the hope of finding water, but always in vain.

Experiments carried out in England by Mr. Barrett (see *Sanitary Record*, 2 May, 1923) gave similar results.

In another experiment, two operators using the divining rod found the exact location of five metal plates which had been wrapped in paper and buried in a field. The five plates were all of different composition. Not only were all five located, but both operators working independently and at different times were able to name the metals correctly and their results tallied exactly. Different metals can be told apart by the fact that some appear to influence the rod much more strongly than others. From the above remarks, it would appear that water or metals in some strange manner affect the divining rod when it is held in the hands of certain specially gifted individuals.

We can eliminate the hypothesis of chance. The experiments, moreover, were carried out in such a way as to leave very little room for the possibility of fraud. The rod moves in the hands of the operator without any interference on his part. The manner in which it moves and the intensity of motion give indications as to depth in the case of water, but it naturally takes an experienced user to get good results.

There are two possible explanations. Either the movement of the rod is due to unconscious muscular contraction, or the movement of the rod is entirely independent of any muscular contraction. The first alternative seems the most acceptable, but there are considerable difficulties to be faced. The movements of the rod are sometimes strong enough to break it. Those portions of the rod that lie within the hands of the operator do not move. If the ends of the rod are encased in hollow containers, which are held by the operator, the rod twists and moves within the casing.

If we take the above facts as sufficient evidence to prove that the movement of the rod is not due to muscular action, we must conclude that water and metals exert strong direct physical force on the rod.

But if this were really the case there would be no need for a human operator. If the rod was part of a mechanical instrument showing angular deviation, the same results would be obtained. But this is not so. Attempts to construct such instruments have invariably resulted in failure.

We can only conclude therefore that the movement is due to unconscious muscular action on the part of the operator.

In other words, buried masses of metal or hidden subterranean streams exert some mysterious influence which sensitive human beings can perceive under certain conditions, and considered in this light, the phenomenon comes naturally under the heading of cryptesthesis. I have described it at some length in this chapter as throwing a curious light on the subject of motor automatism.

We can summarise our conclusions as follows: –

The numerous methods applied for purposes of divination can be described as purely conventional, and artificial practices based on traditional observations and analogy, with the exception of sensory and motor automatism, which, though by no means free from fraud, appear to have a foundation of truth, depending on the faculty of cryptesthesis.

We now come to a process of divination essentially different from any we have mentioned hitherto. It belongs to the class of heteroscopic methods, but is considered as a science in itself.

Astrology was not only the ancient art of divining the fate and future of human beings from indications given by the positions of the stars, it was also a belief in an intimate connection between the heavenly bodies and the life of men. I shall return to this subject of astrology when dealing with magic, and will only mention it here on account of its divinatory aspect. Astrology is very old, it is the earliest of all sciences, and the grandparent of astronomy in the same way as alchemy preceded chemistry. The Chaldeans were the greatest astronomers or astrologers of antiquity, but forms of astrology and a rudimentary knowledge of the heavenly bodies can be found earlier even than 3000 b.c.

As far as we can tell at the present day, astrology is mere superstition; there is certainly nothing as yet to connect it with any of the results obtained by modern investigators.

Starting with the indisputable fact that man's life and happiness are largely dependent on the heavens, the sun shining, the rains and floods, and the fertility of the soil, it was a natural step to assume that the life of man was influenced by, and connected with, the movement of the heavenly bodies.

I have shown that the sun and moon, and later the planets, were gods and objects of worship from being originally considered as the heavenly prototypes of human life on earth.

In the hands of the Greeks and of the later Egyptians, both astrology and astronomy were carried far beyond the limits attained by the Babylonians, and the harmony between them continued until the threshold of modem science was reached in the sixteenth century.

The endeavour to trace the horoscope of the individual from the position of the planets and stars at the time of his birth or at the time of conception represents the most significant contribution of the Greeks to astrology. The system was carried to such a degree of perfection that later ages made but few additions.

The system was taken up almost bodily by the Arabs, and calculations based on astronomical data were introduced into the Kabala by the Jews. In further development of views unfolded in Babylonia, the scope of astrology was extended until it was brought into connection with practically all of the known sciences – botany, chemistry, zoology, mineralogy, anatomy, and medicine.

The world-old principle of analogy caused colours, stones, plants, drugs, and animal life of all kinds to be associated with the planets and under their tutelage.

Astrology in its earliest stage is marked by two characteristic limitations. In the first place, the movements and positions of the heavenly bodies point to such occurrences as are of public import and affect the general welfare; in the second place, the astronomical knowledge is essentially empirical. While in a general way the reign of law and order in the movement of the heavenly bodies was recognised, and indeed must have exercised an influence at an early period in leading to the rise of a methodical divination that was certainly of a much higher order than the examination of an animal's liver, yet the importance that was laid upon the endless variations in the form of the phenomena, and the equally numerous apparent deviations from what were regarded as normal conditions, prevented for a long time the rise of any serious study of astronomy beyond what was needed for the purely practical purposes that the priests as 'inspectors' of the heavens had in mind (*Enc. Brit.* Astr.). Astrology is of no real interest to us as a process of divination, we will find that its true import lies in its connection with magic.

The predictions of certain astrologers have appeared remarkably accurate, but once again this is no proof of the value of astronomical predictions. The more famous astrologers, such as Nostradamus, were most certainly gifted with cryptesthesic power, and subject to monitions and premonitions. The prevalence of astrology and its importance are due to its connection with Magic, and consequently with Black Magic, and to the fact also that the sun, the moon, and the planets were originally religious symbols, visible expressions of the theory of life, and later the deities. The symbol itself was worshipped in place of the idea it stood for, and the belief in the influence of the heavenly bodies on mankind was a natural one, since the heavenly bodies were to all intents and purposes gods.

In conclusion, we may say that the rites and practices of divination were purely conventional and entirely artificial, but cryptesthesis has proved to us that such a thing as divination is not only possible but fairly frequently met with.

We must conclude therefore that although the practices and rites may have been vain, the soothsayer sometimes possessed that mysterious gift which enables man to perceive things to which the normal senses cannot respond, which mediums and hypnotic subjects possess to an extraordinary degree, which normal individuals sometimes experience under the form of monitions and premonitions, and which is known to modern science as cryptesthesis.

This conception may not appear so strange if we reason by analogy; let us assume a world wherein every man, with the exception of a small number of abnormal beings, was devoid of the sense of smell, although possessing the faculties of sight and touch; let us suppose that a normal man of this community was walking down a lane between two high walls, accompanied by one of these gifted individuals; the latter, smelling strawberries, for instance, growing on the far side of the wall, would be able to say to his companion that such fruit were to be found there. He would be quite unable to convey to his companion's mind the way in which he had become aware of the fact, since a sense of smell cannot be described to one who has never possessed it, and the performance would appear quite inexplicable by ordinary natural laws.

It is the same with cryptesthesis; it is a sixth sense, which some individuals seem to possess although they cannot explain its nature to us. It is to a certain extent latent in the majority of human beings, and perhaps at some future date means will be found whereby it may be developed.

CHAPTER X

ALCHEMY

'Si tu veux faire un metal, prends un metal; car un chien n'est jamais engendré que par un chien.'

Le Cosmopolite.

O f all branches of occult science, perhaps alchemy has had the greater number of devotees. Its object is sufficient reason for its popularity. Some three thousand volumes have been written on the subject, and most of these are folio size, while a number of clever and educated men have devoted the whole of their lives to the pursuit of the Philosopher's Stone.

While alchemy afforded the most admirable opportunities for swindlers and impostors of every description, it was by no means entirely fraudulent. Alchemy is a very complex subject, and the ideas and principles on which it is based are far older and more general in their bearings and applications than is usually supposed.

Considered superficially, alchemy, like astrology, is a science of transition between a period when the animistic system prevailed, when all natural phenomena were controlled by gods and spirits, and a later period, the era of scientific positivism. Positive facts crept into the original forms, and we thus find a curious blending of scientific facts and mystic rites.

It is very tempting to consider alchemy solely in this way and trace it to its apparent origin through its analogy with astrology, the gradual progression from the animistic to the scientific. The idea is seductive, and plausible, and has been adopted without further examination by a number of investigators. But, if such a conception of alchemy does contain in fact a large proportion of the truth, it is unfortunately incomplete, and leads to entirely misleading and fallacious conclusions.

That such a transitory tendency may have influenced the form of alchemy I am fully prepared to admit, but the true meaning of alchemy, as I hope to show, is to be found in the old tri-unal doctrine of which the triad is the symbol.

Before we examine the origins and esoteric meaning of alchemy, however, it will be well to obtain an idea of the facts relating to it.

Alchemy, in the narrowest sense of the word, was the name given to the art of transmuting the baser metals into gold. More generally and correctly, alchemy meant 'the purification of matter' in its different forms, mineral, vegetable, and animal, the object being attained by means of the philosopher's stone in the one case, by the universal panacea or Elixir of Life in the others.

My object in this chapter will be to prove the following statements: –

(1)   That alchemy can be traced back to the oldest records of Egyptian knowledge, and was but a form or part

of the tri-unal doctrine that lies at the root of all initiatic rites. Philosophical or mystic initiation being based on a tri-unal theogony, from which a tri-unal androgony was derived by analogy, which itself gave rise to Phallic and nature cults; a tri-unal cosmogony was similarly evolved, and this constitutes the root principle of Hermetic Science, or alchemy.

(2)   That although we cannot accept the evidence of actual transmutations accomplished in the past, however genuine such cases may appear to be, yet the principle underlying alchemy, leaving aside philosophical or religious considerations, is a true one and almost identical to modem theories concerning the constitution of matter.

(3)   That the mystery and obscurity surrounding alchemy arc due to the symbolism used by the initiates, which symbolism is directly derived from the triad, on the one hand, to the introduction into the practice of alchemy proper of the more spectacular phenomena of early chemical science, on the other hand, and finally to the appearance of countless impostors and to the corruption of original alchemical practices through the contagion of Sorcery and Black Magic.

The earliest Hermetic writers describe three distinct forms of the art. Metallurgy, or the art of extracting metals from the soil; the preparation of alloys, closely resembling gold, or the art of apparently increasing a given amount of gold by blending it with silver, etc.; alchemy proper, or the creation of pure gold, or rather transmutation of a baser metal into gold.

The third form, or true alchemy, is the only one which need retain our attention, the other two belong to the realm of chemistry.

There are a few outstanding cases amongst the more recent experiments which may be picked out from the immense collection of facts relating to alchemy, and I have thought it of interest to reproduce these in order that the reader may get a clear idea of the nature of these facts and of the evidence that has been put forward in the defence of alchemy. These cases have been chosen for four reasons. Firstly, in all three cases the alchemist was not present during the experiment. Secondly, he was given no opportunity of touching or interfering with any of the apparatus or materials used. Thirdly, the results obtained cannot be explained by any law known to modern chemistry. Fourthly, the experimenter was in all three cases a well-known scientific investigator entirely hostile to alchemical practice.

The first of these cases concerns Helvetius, and the date of the occurrence is 1666. John Frederc Schweitzer, better known as Helvetius, was one of the most persistent among the adversaries of alchemy. On the 27th of December, 1666, at the Hague he received a visit from a stranger, dressed after the fashion of a Dutch merchant, and who obstinately refused to reveal his name. The stranger stated that he had come to Helvetius in order to give him proof of the possibility of transmutation, and convince him of the error of his antagonistic attitude. During a long conversation he upheld the hermetic doctrine, and finally showed to Helvetius a small ivory box containing a reddish powder which, he stated, was the philosopher's stone.

Helvetius begged of him to give him a demonstration of its powers, but in vain, and the stranger left him after promising to return in three weeks' time. While he was talking Helvetius had been skilful enough to secrete a small amount of the powder under his finger-nail, and as soon as the stranger left him he proceeded to his laboratory and, melting a small amount of lead in a crucible, he threw the powder into the molten mass.

The experiment, however, was a complete failure, the powder was instantaneously vaporised and the lead remained unchanged. Believing the man to be an impostor, Helvetius had well-nigh forgotten the incident, when the stranger returned as promised at the end of three weeks. He again refused to conduct any experiment himself, but gave Helvetius a small quantity of the powder, about the size of a grain of millet, and told him that it was essential that the powder should be enclosed in some protective casing before being dropped into the molten metal. Helvetius then understood the reason for his early failure. Alone in his laboratory, he melted an ounce and a half of lead in a crucible, enclosed the powder within a wax pellet, and, dropping it into the crucible, left it on the fire for a short time. When the crucible was examined the metal showed the particular rich grey hue of molten gold, and on being allowed to cool was found to consist of a block of yellow metal, apparently gold. All the goldsmiths of the Hague examined this metal and pronounced it to be the purest gold. Povelius, chief tester for the Dutch mint, tested it no less than seven times and found it absolutely pure.

Helvetius was so impressed that he wrote his *Vitulus Aureus*, in which this experiment is described and the object of which is to uphold the cause of alchemy.

We find interesting confirmation of this event in a letter written by Spinoza to Jarrig Jellis: –

'Having spoken to Voss about the Helvetius experiment he laughed at me, and in order to set my mind at rest I went to see the goldsmith Bretchel who had tested the gold. He assured me that it was pure gold. Not only Bretchel, but many other people who had witnessed the tests assured me that it was pure gold. I then called on Helvetius, who showed me the gold and the crucible, around the sides of which small particles of gold could still be seen adhering. He told me that the amount of powder he had used was equivalent to the quarter of a grain of corn, and that he would let the whole world hear of this experiment. It would seem that this adept had already conducted a similar experiment in Amsterdam and was still to be found in that town.

'Boorbourg, 27th March, 1667.'
(Spinoza, *Opera Posthuma*, p. 553.)

The second case is taken from an account by Berigord de Pise. 'I will write,' says he, 'what occurred at a time when I doubted the possibility of transmuting mercury into gold. A certain person, wishing to dispel my doubts on the subject, gave me some powder, the colour of which was like wild poppies and the smell like burned sea-salt. In order to avoid any chance of fraud, I myself bought a new crucible, and even the coal and mercury all from different merchants, and was then sure there could be no gold hidden within the crucible or the mercury, which is a common trick with impostors. To ten units of mercury I added a little powder and heated the crucible for some time, after which I found the mercury had been transmuted into an equivalent weight of a yellow metal which, on being carefully and repeatedly tested, was proved to be pure gold. If this experiment had not been carried out by myself alone in the absence of any witnesses, I would have suspected some fraud, but under the circumstances no such possibility arose.'

Here again we are in the presence of a case where a learned man, used to experimental work, a disbeliever in alchemy, and, moreover, a man who is well aware of the tricks employed by impostors, conducts a successful experiment and is convinced.

The third case is that of Van Helmont. In 1618, in his laboratory near Vilvorde, in the neighbourhood of Brussels, Van Helmont was given a quarter of a grain of the powder by a stranger. Van Helmont carried out the experiment when alone in his laboratory. With the amount of powder given to him he transmuted into gold eight ounces of mercury. Van Helmont was possibly the greatest chemist of his time, a philosopher and an adversary of alchemy. The experiment appeared so convincing to him that he spent the rest of his life trying to find the stone, but in vain.

These three cases are very curious, none of the operators believed in alchemy, all of them were noted chemists, and in no case had the alchemist anything to do with the experiment, or any contact whatsoever with the materials used. Moreover, in the case of Berigord de Pise, if the mercury had contained any gold, which might be left over after the mercury was driven off as a vapour, the amount of gold left could not have been equivalent in weight to that of the original amount of mercury.

Such is the case for the defence of alchemy, but curious as the facts may be, and there are innumerable others of similar nature, the evidence is too old and uncertain for any statement to be made one way or the other. One cannot help wondering at the mysterious nature of the adept who appears in all three cases and then vanishes when those he has approached have been convinced.

The principle underlying alchemy, the unity of matter, is an accepted theory in a sense today, but the possibility of transmutation without the liberation or absorption of huge quantities of energy seems more remote than ever. We are not, however, so much concerned with the possibility of transmutation as with the origin of alchemy and its relation to occult science.

The cases we have just examined show us alchemy proper in the hands of sincere and scientific investigators, but alchemy is more frequently met with under a different form, the pastime of the rich, the golden opportunity of the swindler, already tainted with appended Sorcery and with mystic rites indiscriminately borrowed from Magic. In this form it is truly characteristic of mediaeval times. A truly enormous number of impostors arose who claimed to possess the secret of the philosopher's stone. Considering the fact that in some experiments it was necessary to keep the 'matter' at a constant temperature for fifteen or twenty years they were fairly safe from exposure, and at the worst these parasites obtained board and lodging for years, moving from one patron to another according to their tastes and convenience.

The case of Madame d'Urfé, as related by Casanova in his Memoirs, is a remarkable example of this form of swindle, and no better picture can be drawn of the amateur alchemist than can be found in the account of the adventure that befell this extraordinary woman, an extract of which account I will now give.

'After the dessert Tout d'Auvergne left us to go and see the Prince of Turenne, who was in a high fever, and after he was gone Madame d'Urfé began to discuss alchemy and magic, and all the other branches of her beloved science, or rather infatuation. When we got on to the Magnum Opus, and I asked her if she knew the nature of the first matter, it was only her politeness that prevented her from laughing, but, controlling herself, she replied graciously that she already possessed the philosopher's stone and that she was acquainted with all the operations of the work. She then showed me a collection of books which had belonged to the great d'Urfé and Renee of Savoie, his wife; but she had added to it manuscripts which had cost her more than a hundred thousand francs. Paracelsus was her favourite author, and according to her, he was neither man, woman, nor hermaphrodite, and had the misfortune to poison himself with an overdose of his panacea, or universal medicine. She showed me a manuscript in French where the great work was clearly explained. From the library we went into the laboratory, at which I was truly astonished. She showed me matter that had been in the furnace for fifteen years and was to be there for four or five more. It was a powder of projection which was to transform instantaneously all metals into the finest gold. She showed me a pipe by which the coal descended to the furnace, always keeping it at the same heat. The lumps of coal were impelled by their own weight at proper intervals and in equal quantities so that she was often three months without looking at the furnace, the temperature remaining the same the whole time. The calcination of mercury was mere child's play to this wonderful woman. She showed me the calcinated matter and said that whenever I liked she would instruct me as to the process. I next saw the Tree of Diana of the famous Tahamed, whose pupil she was. His real name was Maillot, and according to Madame d'Urfé he had not, as was supposed, died at Marseilles, but was still alive; 'and,' added she with a slight smile, 'I often get letters from him. If the Regent of France had listened to me he would be alive now. He was my first friend; he gave me the name of Egeria, and he married me to Monsieur d'Urfé,' She possessed a commentary on Raymond Lulli which cleared up all difficulties in the comments of Arnold de Villanova on the work of Roger Bacon and Heber, who, according to her, were still alive. This precious manuscript was in an ivory casket, the key of which she kept religiously. Indeed, her laboratory was a closed room to all but myself. I saw a small cask full of Platina del Pinto which she told me she could transmute to gold when she pleased. It had been given to her by Vood himself in 1743. She showed me the same metal in four phials. In the first three the platinum remained intact, in sulphuric acid, nitric acid, and muriatic acid; but in the fourth, which contained *aqua regia*, the metal had not been able to resist the action of the acid. She melted it with the burning glass and said it could not be melted in any other way, which proved, in her opinion, its superiority over gold. She showed me some she had precipitated by sal ammoniac, which would not precipitate gold. Her athanor had been alight for fifteen years, the top was covered with black coal, which made me conclude that she had been in the laboratory two or three days before. Stopping before the Tree of Diana, I asked her in a respectful voice if she agreed with those who said it was only fit to amuse children. She replied in a dignified manner that she had made it to divert herself with the crystallisation of the silver, spirit of nitre, and mercury, and that she only looked upon it as a piece of metallic vegetation representing in little what Nature performed on a larger scale, but she added very seriously that she could make a tree of Diana that should be a very Tree of the Sun, which would produce golden fruit which might be gathered and which would continue to be produced till no more remained of a certain ingredient. I said modestly that I could not believe the thing possible without the powder of projection, but her only answer was a pleased smile.'

Thus did the adepts of alchemy waste their lives and fortunes in a frantic search for the philosopher's stone. In many cases, however, the practices of alchemy were not so innocent or harmless. When every ingredient had been used, when prayers and incantations had proved unavailing, when the long and arduous research had become first an obsession and then a form of madness, the curtain rose on scenes indescribable. The rarer manuscripts concerning Sorcery and Magic, those few that have escaped destruction, abound in scenes of horror and unrestrained bestiality, but some of the more corrupt forms of alchemy are unsurpassed in this respect. I regret that conventions make it impossible to more than hint at the nature of these practices, for in spite of their horror they are of quite remarkable interest, and it is difficult without them to get a correct impression of the corrupted form of alchemy that was prevalent from the fifteenth to the seventeenth century.

The case of Gilles de Rais is a typical example. He was a sadist and a madman, but his infirmities and his greed for gold were skilfully exploited by impostors and parasites without whose pernicious influence he might never have been driven to those monstrous crimes which brought him to the stake.

This form of alchemy is, however, by no means universal. With Raymond Lulli, for instance, alchemy is a pure science, with Paracelsus it takes a more general form, and the Elixir of Life becomes the object of the quest. Hermetic science in its broadest acceptation is only a cosmogonic form of a far more general doctrine. Berthelot, the great French chemist, in his Origins of Alchemy, came very near the truth when he made the following statement:

'L'alchimie pretendait a la fois enrichir les adeptes en leur apprenant a fabriquer de For, les mettre a l'abri des malaxes par la preparation de la panacee, eniin leur procurer le bonheur parfait en les identifiant avec l'Sme du monde et l'esprit universel.'

The true aim of all initiations was to perfect or purify the being by a gradual process, until such a time as the adept attained perfect wisdom, after which he passed from the material world never to return. This doctrine was obviously inseparable from the doctrine of reincarnation which is common under various forms to all the older religions and primitive beliefs. In other words, perfection could not be attained in one life, but the initiates believed in reincarnation, not only in animal but in vegetable and even in mineral form, in the very early stages of progression, and the ' soul of matter ' was the universal basic principle from which matter is derived. Alchemy proper, or the purification of metals, was merely a phase in the progression of the adept, who, when nearing perfect wisdom, was endowed with certain powers over material objects, the transmutation or purification of metals being one of many.

In this respect alchemy is closely related to magic, and the power of transmuting metals is amongst those granted to the adept of magic, but the purification and transmutation of alchemy is really an analogy, almost a symbol, of that great purification of the being which was the aim of initiation. The symbolism used in alchemical writings and the form of the operations described are so closely related to the symbolism to be found at the root of all religious systems that there can be no doubt as to the identity of purpose.

We have already examined the Androgonic expression of the tri-unal doctrine, or body-soul-spirit triangle combined with the four elements, water, fire, earth, and air. These geometrical figures exactly correspond to those used by alchemists to express the completed work, or philosopher's stone, thus ⊽. The sulphur of alchemists was the expression of the spirit as free from or dominating matter, its symbol being ⚴.

The triangle inscribed within a square itself enclosed in a circle was a synthetic expression of the world, spirit enclosed within matter, together with the idea of continuity.

The various alchemical figures or symbols always contain a triangle, the 'sulphur' or active principle ♯ and the 'salt' ⊖ or passive principle, together with the 'mercury' ☿ or binding principle.

The symbolism is strikingly similar to that studied in Chapter II. 'Sulphur ' was used merely as a word symbolical of fire, or the sun, or the active principle. The female principle was ' Salt,' or nature, or water (the sea), or moon, and the binding principle was called 'Mercury,' presumably because mercury actually seemed to be an intermediate form between the metal or solid, and the liquid, thus partaking of both. It is particularly interesting to note that the symbol for mercury was always the symbol of the hermaphrodite, which is only another form of Androgyne.

Sulphur ♯, Mercury ☿ and Salt ⊖, Fire △, Air ◮, Water ▽, and Earth ▿, such are the symbols of the three principles and four elementary forms of matter.

The sulphur is the fire, the creative principle; the salt the basic foundation and origin of all matter; and alchemy is seen to be nothing but a cosmogonic form or application of the old tri-unal doctrine. The names Sulphur, Mercury, and Salt were, of course, only used symbolically, and had no reference to the actual sulphur, etc., of nature. The alchemical doctrine can be briefly stated as follows:

Matter is all 'one.' All metals, for instance, are composed of sulphur and mercury in variable quantities, and these two principles are condensed or materialised by means of a salt. The various quantities of one or other of these three principles is the cause of differences between one metal and another. Metals are the fruits of mineral nature, they are more or less ripe. The baser metals are unripe fruit, that have been cut from the tree of life before the sulphur and mercury have combined and ripened in the right proportions. The philosopher's stone is a ferment that ripens or hurries on the progressive processes of nature, and hence transmutes baser metal into gold.

Now it is easy to see throughout all this obscure symbolism that the idea is the same as the progression or purification of man through consecutive reincarnations. The baser metals correspond to the lowest type of man, and the philosopher's stone hurries on the perfecting process of nature, just as the panacea saves the human body from all ills, or the philosophical initiation saves the soul from the domination of matter. It is only a question of var5ring planes, the idea is alwa3rs the same. The quest of the mystic was spiritual gold, or the identification of human intelligence with the divine essence. The common aim is the attainment of a higher degree along a natural scale of progression, either for a metal, for the human body, or for the human soul; the system is either a cosmogony, an androgony, or a theogony. In either case it corresponds to the general law of evolution. Alchemy was a natural consequence of the trinity, the extension of a single master-system to cover philosophy, life, and nature.

The Tabula Smaragdina, attributed to Hermes Trismagistus, is a very striking example of this symbolism. It can be taken either as the expression of a philosophical doctrine, or as the symbolical description of the Magnum Opus of alchemy, Hermes was considered by alchemists as the father and originator of the science. We still use to this day the expression ' hermetically sealed,' which is a relic of the time when all ingredients were kept in flasks, on the wax seals of which the seal of Hermes was impressed. The ancient Egyptians practised alchemy both in its purely metallurgical form and in its true form. The Papyri of Leide, found in a tomb at Thebes, confirm this point beyond any possibility of doubt. Alchemy was part of the secret Egyptian initiations, and was practised exclusively by the priests.

As a further example of this symbolism we may quote the following from Stephanus:

'In order to attain perfection, the soul must be drawn from matter, separated from the body. Copper is like a man, it has a soul and a material body. . . . Which is the body and which is the soul? The soul is that which is more subtle or volatile, the body is that which has weight and is material and can cast a shadow. By a number of suitable operations, copper loses its body and becomes finer than gold.'

This is clearly an analogy to the philosophical doctrine.

The symbolism varies somewhat according to the period and the country, and is often purely religious, the gods that have been created to personify the principles expressed by the ideal triad replace the simpler symbols used in the earlier forms. Thus the sun and moon are used very naturally to express the essence and the materiality of matter. Osiris and his tomb, Isis and Horus, are all used as symbols to express the same ideas, thus making the analogy even more complete. It is in this sense, of course, that the Androgyne is so often pictured in alchemical writings. A figure male on one side and female on the other. It is a pictorial expression of the triad. On the man's breast we find the sign of sulphur, on the woman's breast the sign of salt, and on the navel, common to both, the sign of mercury, thus completing the triangle. The Androgyne in this form is an alchemical symbol; we have seen identical figures devoid of the alchemical signs widely used as symbols of nature or sex worship, and the hermaphrodite is only another form of the same symbol, the characteristic sign for which is also that of mercury.

At a later period the alchemists abandoned the primitive simplicity of their doctrines as chemical facts became known, and the growth of chemistry within the realm of alchemy explains the complexity of the later symbols as compared with those of the earliest operators.

CHAPTER XI

THE ARCANAS OF INITIATIC MAGIC

'Vouloir sans desirer, voilà le secret de la puissance.'
Eliphas Levi.

Magic in its true sense we have defined as the inner, more secret doctrine to be found behind the outer forms and ceremonies of the early religions. Around this initiatic creed legends grew, fostered by superstition and ignorance, till the word magic came to embrace Sorcery and Witchcraft, in a word, every branch of what has been so vaguely termed the occult. Whereas Witchcraft and Black Magic, mainly on account of their inherent criminal practices, gained rapid notoriety, and, being constantly before the eyes of men, entered into their very lives. Magic has always remained truly occult in this sense, that its practices and teachings were restricted to the very few, and it was and still is confined to certain initiatic brotherhoods and utterly unknown to the world at large.

For this very reason this aspect of occult science has been too often ignored, and an analysis of witchcraft and certain primitive religious ceremonies taken as a complete representation of the magical lore of the past.

Magic is a religion; it is more than a mere religion, since it embodies the fundamental principles common to all religions. It is in fact the direct interpretation of the trinity in its most abstract form. Just as religions gradually developed into intricate and elaborate systems, so Magic also evolved from its original simple form. But, with this difference; Magic has its demonology, in the same way as religion, but in the case of Magic the demonology is the result of the analysis of a fundamental creed, whereas religion is the synthesis of demonology. This elaboration of Magic is only apparent; it is often due to a deliberate intention to mislead. Magic proper was of so secret a nature, and such was the importance attached to its secrets, that the whole creed from the earliest traces of its existence has been protected from the investigations of the curious either by the total absence of any material documents or by the use of a symbolism and language so obscure as to discourage the most tenacious searchers.

The elaborate ceremonial prescribed is an example of this characteristic mystification, and the numerous ramifications of Magic are so complex that it is almost impossible to discriminate between that which is truly symbolical and that which has been added in later times and may therefore be considered as a corruption of the true original doctrine. Here again we have to consider the influence of Witchcraft and Black Magic and the innumerable superstitions and beliefs that arose at various periods; we have to consider the influence of divination, astrology, and alchemy, parts of which belong to Magic proper. Many of the devotees of these practices, whether charlatans or sincere investigators, claimed to be adepts of Magic, and this affords some clue to the reason for which Initiatic Magic was not recognised as a separate entity but generally confused with other forms of the occult. There are few writings that refer to genuine Magic. By far the greater number are the work of alchemists or mystics, philosophers or theologists, and amongst the complicated theories and systems they expound the slender thread of the initiatic doctrine is exceedingly difficult to follow.

Since Magic is based on the fundamental trinity, its symbolism naturally coincides with the symbolism common to all religions and also to alchemy. This symbolism we have already defined. Magic was the development along purely abstract lines of the original trinitarian doctrine. It can be traced without interruption through the various religions of the world. One cannot help but be struck by the very evident importance of initiatic rites in such countries as Egypt, or among the Hebrews, while we have seen that symbolism was the direct outcome of these initiations, afterwards elaborated and modified, according to the modifications of the original creed.

It is a matter of some considerable difficulty to determine just what initiation meant. There is every reason to believe, however, that its fundamental principles, both as regards the object to be attained and the means of attainment, were the same in every case, although the forms of ceremonial and ritual observed may have been very different.

The solemn and austere character of what little we know of the Egyptian rites is obviously not in keeping with that of the Mysteries of Eleusis; yet there is much evidence to prove that the final object of achievement was in both cases identical. The question is further complicated by the early appearance and rapid growth of such cults as Phallic worship, with the result that in a great many cases it is impossible to tell whether the object of these rites was purely Phallic or whether the deeper meaning was still present and the rites, in this sense, truly initiatic.

When we come to consider the object of the rites in itself, the secret and true nature of initiation, we find that the very simplicity of the ideas conveyed is the greatest obstacle to their proper comprehension.

Initiation was more destructive than constructive, on account of the very simplicity of its tenets. It is in this sense, perhaps, that we should understand the awe with which it was regarded and the safeguards that were taken against its premature revelation. It has been compared to a blinding fight, so bright that the majority cannot perceive it, the blinding fight of truth, and these various analogies point to the revelation of an idea so simple and yet so obviously true that one insufficiently prepared would fail to understand its beauty and universal character. The attainment of an imperfect degree of knowledge and philosophy would result in such a revelation merely stressing the futility of acquired facts, and for initiation to be a fitting stone wherewith to crown the edifice it was required that this should be both perfect and complete. This culmination of acquired wisdom was of such a nature as to be destructive in a mental sense to such as were unable to grasp fully its true character, whereas it provided a path towards an eventually perfect state of wisdom for those who proved worthy of the achievement.

We have examined the probable nature of the initiatic secret in the first chapter of these essays, as well as the reasons for which it was considered as a universal truth, and the key to immortal wisdom through a succession of fives, not necessarily spent on earth, but in each of which man found himself a stage nearer to, or a stage further from, perfection according to the nature of his actions in the preceding one. The idea of good, or the conception of what a man's actions in life should be, was not based on any artificial code; the aim of man's life was to attain wisdom, and the unforgivable sin was neglect of the gifts and opportunities afforded him. This conception exists in almost identical form in the Buddhist religion, as the various degrees of Ahratship, for instance, while we find many striking examples of it in the teachings of Christ; the parable of the talents is perhaps the clearest reference to be found in the New Testament.

There was a further aspect to be found in the initiatic idea, prior to the final revelation, a more objective form which has also left its mark on many religious systems. The belief in the supreme power of will over matter, of which the Yogist creed is a typical example, can be considered as the very foundation of initiatic doctrines. The acquirement of this power was the object of the long preparatory stages of initiation, and the rites preceding the actual revelation of the ultimate secret were intended as a trial to determine the extent of this power in the neophyte.

Herein we find another reason to explain the numerous references to the dangerous nature of initiation. In this connection the danger was physical, and insufficient preparation or any faltering meant death. As in the case of the Yogist sect, and that of a considerable number of similar systems from the Fakirs of India to the Aisaouas and

Derviches of Arabia, self-hypnotism played a predominant part in the production of various states of trance.

This state of auto-hypnotism is a common feature of certain cults, and can be carried to extremes. It is induced by special forms of dancing in the cruder form, and by a pure effort of will in the more advanced forms such as Yogism. In the early phases the patient appears to be quite immune from pain, and, curiously enough, no wounds, abrasions, or burns appear upon his body. I have personally seen members of the Aisaoua sect, in Kairouan, place blazing bundles of straw under their arms and leave them there till nothing but ash remained; yet their skins showed no sign of burning whatsoever. There are innumerable examples of similar practices to be found in various parts of the world, and there appears to be no attempt at fraud, at any rate so far as those that have come under my personal observation are concerned.

In the later phases the state of trance becomes cataleptic and we get such effects as have been observed in India when patients have been buried under the ground for weeks and have afterwards revived. During this phase the initiates of old believed that their spirit, or, more correctly, their astral body, was free to go where it would, not only on earth but in other planes, and it was while in a state of trance that Isis was approached by the initiates, one of the most dreaded mysteries of the inner sanctuary.

Magic in its more familiar forms has its elaborate ceremonials and its apparently purposeless ritual. It invokes a host of spirits, the names of which are carefully recorded; it possesses astrological practices of its own, and is closely connected with both alchemy and divination; it has its vestments, prayers and altar, and much of the paraphernalia that is associated with charlatanism. The Magus lays claims to powers which are quite evidently absurd. The traditions of demonology and the ever-present belief in the existence of beings of another world are important features of Magic. The nature of these beings, however, is quite different from that of the demons and spirits of other creeds and is perfectly well defined in the various rituals. They were of two distinct types: a group of beings instinctively inimical to man, of very inferior intellect, and of a bestial nature, but dominated and enslaved by the magician, and a group of spiritual beings or spirits of light, friendly to man, of very superior intelligence, corresponding to the angels of Christianity. The former were known as elemental spirits and were closely associated with the four forms of matter – earth, fire, water, and air. They were correspondingly divided into Gnomes, Slamanders, Undines, and Sylphs. The object of invocation rites was to call up and materialise these elemental spirits in order that they might be made to serve some predetermined purpose.

All this, however, is but the outer form. We have already pointed out the misleading character of writings on Magic and the deliberate mystification that was loyally kept up for the purpose of discouraging the merely curious. The greater part of the ceremonial is symbolical, and was never intended for use. The names of the spirits and demons hide carefully concealed abstract ideas, and the powers claimed by the Magi are only subtle expressions for powers of a very different nature.

Nevertheless the ceremonial form of Magic is of great interest because on careful analysis it reveals the fact that apart from its inherent symbolism its every detail was devised for the express purpose of obtaining intense concentration and the development of will power. It is highly probable that in this respect a certain portion of the ritual was actually used during the early periods of initiation, to be gradually left aside as the novice grasped the true meaning it was intended to convey. Much of the ritual was drawn up with a view to creating atmosphere, and the burning of carefully selected herbs was intended to encourage a visionary state.

It was precisely this mass of seemingly meaningless ceremonies that was taken literally by the adepts of Black Magic. The demons were taken as real entities, and the powers claimed anxiously sought after. The invocation rites were performed in full ceremonial form; no detail was omitted; the participants stood within an inverted magic circle at the dead of night in some dark solitude, and, enveloped in the smoke of dangerous drugs, worked themselves up to such a pitch of fear and excitement that every shadow became a hideous demon, and in many cases they fled screaming from the spot.

Both the ceremonial of Magic and the names of some of its demons and spirits have become familiar to us on account of this wholesale adoption of its outer forms by the devotees of the black art.

Traces can be found in some of the practices of Sorcery of the methods used by the Magi to ensure concentration of the mind. When a man desired anything and appealed to the sorcerer for help it would obviously not have suited the latter's purpose to disclose to him that if his desire was strong enough he would probably himself find the means of attaining his objective. The sorcerer would tell him, for instance, to rise from his bed every night two hours after midnight, and going into the graveyard, to pluck a handful of some plant and deposit it on the church steps. If the man wanted a thing sufficiently to perform such a complicated and comfortless rite it was more than probable that this fact alone, together with a certain blind faith, would bring about the desired result. If, on the other hand, he omitted to do so on one single night the sorcerer could not be blamed in the event of failure.

The long and elaborate instructions given in the rituals of Magic served no other purpose than this; and clearly as the novice progressed and learned to use his will, as he acquired the inestimable gift of concentration, much of these details, if not the whole of them, could be dispensed with.

Of the final object of this concentration and will power we can say but little. The Magi certainly believed in the existence of elemental spirits and in the possibility of using them for a purpose, or driving them away in cases of haunting or possession. The power of the will over the body was applied for obtaining phenomena such as cryptesthesis with the consequent possibility of becoming aware of events occurring in distant spots. Hypnotism was a further branch of the art, and astrology, divination, and alchemy were all derivations from the same root.

The true achievement of the Magus, however, was a thorough knowledge of life and psychology, the attainment of that form of wisdom and, ultimately, happy philosophy which has found subtle expression in Buddha's smile. The Magus believed that a state of wisdom and absolute self-control would endow him with power, and that through reincarnation he would gradually perfect this state until he could eventually control inanimate objects and the destinies of man. We find proof of this in the purely benevolent nature of Magic and in the fact that the Magus would never use what powers he might possess to increase his material prosperity or add to his well-being. To will without desire was the aim of Magic and the secret of absolute power.

Mutual help, both moral and material, was one of the immediate results of initiation. It is in this respect that Magic carried within itself the germs that were to cause degeneration and ultimate destruction. Just as corruptions of the original creed, or rather, perhaps, the growing importance of the symbol in proportion to its inner meaning, brought about the elaboration of a multitude of religious systems, so with the religion of Initiatic Magic, attempts to revive the priesthoods of very early times resulted in the creation of societies or brotherhoods retaining the original symbolism, but less and less aware of its true meaning as time went on. The idea of mutual help and companionship, which was originally a very secondary consideration, became the main object of the later brotherhoods, a gradual process of degeneration which has been greatly hastened by the rapid development in modern times of commercial and industrial activities. The Freemasons of today jealously guard secrets which they no longer possess, and even in earlier times the Knights Templars and similar associations had been unable to escape from the universal contamination.

The true Magi did not meet in assemblies, they hardly knew one another, they were and are still patient searchers after wisdom and truth; nor did they claim supernatural powers. Their symbolism was that of antiquity, their doctrine mental self-improvement, their method untiring labour, their philosophy fortitude, their object wisdom for themselves, and, eventually, for humanity.

An examination of the ritual of Magic reveals the importance attached to the law of balance and analogy. Many of the strange and apparently illogical details of the ceremonial which have been so strongly criticised will be taken at their proper value when we consider, firstly, that these details and outer forms were purposely introduced into Magic as a blind, and, secondly, that they date back to a time when science was inexistent and were retained in later times on account of their symbolical value.

The tendency to formulate a universal law based on analogies is apparent here as elsewhere, and the Macrocosmos and Microcosmos of Magic are the natural outcome of the considerations we have exposed in an earlier chapter. The initiates believed in a threefold being, composed of a material body, an astral body, and a soul; an active principle, a passive principle, and a directing principle. Both the astral body and the soul survived after death, the former becoming the temporary habitation of the latter until a new life began. The belief in elemental spirits is particularly interesting because of the tendency of certain modem investigators to adopt similar working theories to explain the effects of the 'intelligent forces' of metapsychics. These beings were primarily immaterial, but could materialise under certain specific conditions.

It was believed that they could enter into the bodies of the newly dead, or those temporarily vacated during catalepsy, and possession, vampirism, and a number of similar beliefs were explained in this way.

These spirits were also believed to materialise if some means was afforded them of creating for themselves a temporary semi-material body. The emanation or 'aura' of fresh blood, for instance, was supposed not only to attract elementals but also to cause their partial materialisation. The necessity for the presence either of blood or corpses explains the prevalence of the belief that these spirits haunted graveyards, slaughter-houses, etc.

Earth elementals were believed to be imprisoned within the earth and might be released by such natural cataclysms as earthquakes or landslips, even minor forms of which were supposed to herald the advent of epidemics and other disasters. To this day the inhabitants of certain districts will violently oppose the work of mining engineers or even prospectors owing to the fear that elementals may be released upon the world.

This belief in the existence of elemental spirits, together with a system of will development, constitutes the fundamental basis of the practical or objective side of Magic, the experimental side, as it has sometimes been termed. The attainment of wisdom and mental self-improvement constitutes the doctrinal or philosophical aspect of the creed.

There is no need to describe the ceremonial of Magic, it is familiar to most readers, and the curious will find its details described at very great length in a number of works, the titles of which I have given in the bibliography. The peaked hat and star-spangled robes of the magician are legendary, and so far removed from the true nature of the creed that they can have no place in this chapter. The implements used by the magician – the sword, the trident, the pentacles – were merely ever-present symbols to help him towards concentration. The tracing of the protective magic circle gave a sort of positive reality to his will, and the burning of herbs and preparatory fasts induced a visionary state.

CHAPTER XII

SOME ASPECTS OF
MODERN METAPSYCHICS

'A science dealing with mechanical or psychical phenomena which are due to apparently intelligent forces, or to unknown forces which exist in a latent state within the human intellect.'

Charles Richet.

We have examined Sorcery and Witchcraft, Magic, and various similar beliefs, and, having divested them of their surrounding atmosphere of superstition and legend, having made due allowance for fear and tradition, we have found that we are left with very little that cannot be completely explained in the light of modern scientific knowledge. But we cannot explain all, and this restriction, however small, is sufficient to warrant the conclusion that there is a possibility that in past civilisations more was known about this mysterious something than we know at present. That a very great importance was attached to this in the past we know already, but whether the true initiates of Magic had, or had not, control over what I may call for the present the 'intelligent forces of nature' is a lost secret.

The growth of science in its infancy, and the strange and apparently inexplicable phenomena that were brought to light by experiment or accident, gave new credit to the belief in supernatural agency and fed the records of Magic with new cases, which in due course were handed down to a wondering posterity distorted by well-meaning recorders and commentators beyond recognition.

It has taken the evolution of science and human knowledge through countless ages for investigators to be able to appreciate the fact that there does exist a series of phenomena which can be observed and reproduced, but which, in the present state of our knowledge, we are unable to explain, appearing as it does to lie entirely outside the scope of those laws which govern the better-known forces of nature. It has been the privilege of Charles Richer to sort out from the enormous bulk of records contributed by so-called 'spiritualism' in various countries, the fundamental principles of a new science, which fundamental principles he has set out to demonstrate by ordinary scientific methods without attempting to give any explanation for their occurrence. His energies were confined to the elimination of fraud and personal error, and the facts he has established appear to be beyond any possibility of doubt. The numerous examples given in his *Traité de Metapsychique* are so convincing and precise that they cannot be lightly put aside. He has established the existence of a certain number of clearly defined phenomena, and I propose in this chapter to give the reader some idea of their nature, and of the nature of the evidence that supports the assumption of their existence. A careful study of the book itself is, of course, essential if the reader is to form an opinion for himself, but the present brief outline is given as an indication of the work done and its far-reaching importance.

These phenomena can be divided up into three distinct fundamental groups, which together form the new science of metapsychics.

(1) Cryptesthesis (ancient lucidity), which is a faculty by means of which certain individuals may become aware of facts which cannot be conveyed to their minds by the use of their usual senses.

(2) Telekinesis, that is, a form of mechanical force, different from known mechanical forces, that acts without contact, at a distance and under certain definite conditions upon inanimate objects or persons.

(3) Ectoplasmia (materialisation), that is, the formation of various objects which more often seem to emerge from the human body and assume the appearance of material reality, clothes, veils, living bodies, or portions of bodies.

The main point of divergence between metapsychic phenomena and normal scientific phenomena is a very curious one. Metapsychic phenomena appear to be due to unknown but intelligent forces. Metapsychics can hence be defined as the science of the intelligent forces of nature.

These forces, which are the cause of presentiments, telepathy, movement of objects without material contact, apparitions, and other mechanical and luminous phenomena, do not appear to be governed by invariable laws such as govern physical or chemical phenomena. They appear to have an intelligence of their own, a will of a kind, intentions, which may or may not be human, but which are at any rate akin to human volition.

Metapsychics can again be more generally divided into two distinct parts, objective and subjective metapsychics.

By objective metapsychics we mean such observable manifestations as mechanical, physical, or chemical phenomena. By subjective metapsychics we mean such phenomena as are purely intellectual, and they are more clearly defined by the term cryptesthesis, whereas both telekinesis and ectoplasmia are objective phenomena.

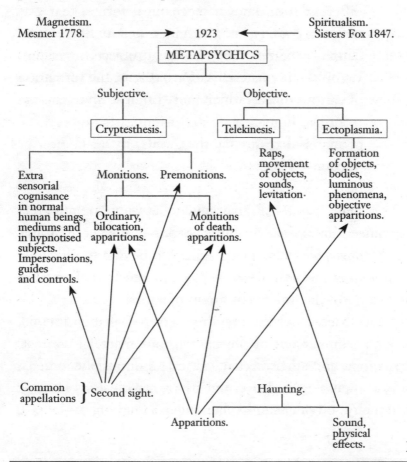

In other words, subjective metapsychics are psychic, non-material, confined to our inner self, whereas objective metapsychics are external and material in their effects.

For example (Richer) in Paris on the 11th of June, 1904, the murder of Queen Draga is foretold by a medium at the very instant it occurred in Belgravia. This is an example of subjective metapsychics. Eusapia Paladino, the famous medium, places her hands fifty centimetres above the surface of a heavy table. Her hands, feet, and knees, waist, head, and mouth are held by reliable scientific witnesses. Under these conditions the table rises into the air, all four feet being simultaneously out of contact with the floor. This is a case of objective metapsychics.

Subjective phenomena are, of course, far more frequently observed than objective phenomena, and, moreover, mediums capable of producing objective phenomena nearly always produce subjective phenomena, whereas the reverse is far from being the case.

The science of metapsychics is much complicated by the fact that it is handicapped at the very start by innumerable experiments that have been wrongly carried out and imperfect observations. Besides this it has been considered by a great many investigators as a religion instead of a science. The side issues of spiritualism have led to a great deal of confusion, and the prevalence of fraud and mystic atmosphere imparted to the proceedings has brought upon them ridicule and doubt. Spiritualists have been so preoccupied with what is 'beyond' that it does not seem to have occurred to them that these phenomena are due perhaps to very real forces of this present world, possibly extended as regards our normal acceptation of the term, but having no relation with anything 'beyond'.

The energies of the investigator should be devoted, not to the unravelling of the possible destiny of man, but, when observing cryptesthesis, for example, to determine whether or not the subject can discover without any hint on the operator's part some thought or fact, to concentrating his whole attention on avoiding any possibility of any such hint being given, or to studying the bearing of the laws of probability on the matter. In the case of an experiment involving telekinesis he should concentrate on securing the medium in such a way as to eliminate fraud, rather than spend his time in vague speculation on the probable nature or immortality of the soul. Theories will quite naturally follow the clear demonstration of the facts, and this should be the first object achieved.

When we state that the forces we are dealing with appear to be intelligent this may, of course, mean that they are purely human, in which case they are produced by some region of the brain, by some phase of human intelligence which we know nothing whatever about.

Historically, Spiritualism can be roughly divided into three periods. The first, or Magnetic period, extends from Mesmer in 1778 to the Fox sisters in 1847; the second, or spiritualistic period, extends from the sisters Fox to Sir William Crookes, 1847-1872; and the third, or scientific period, which extends from Sir William Crookes to the publication of Richet's work in 1923.

One of the main difficulties connected with metapsychical investigations lies in the necessity for employing a medium. There is a considerable difference between such powerful mediums as Home, Eusapia Palladino, Stainton Moses, Florence Cook, and others able to give strong objective phenomena, and other mediums giving only different degrees of subjective phenomena. The former are, moreover, very rarely met with. Unfortunately for the cause of science, the medium is a strange individual. He springs more often from the uneducated classes, and he is usually abnormal in many ways; he seems to have an inherent and often quite unconscious tendency to use fraudulent methods if he is afforded any opportunity of doing so. A medium cannot produce marked phenomena at will, and when his natural gifts fail him he is sorely tempted to supply the deficiency by fraudulent means. Many mediums, moreover, drawing a rich income from their peculiar gifts, have been led into giving regular public seances where fraud was essential in order that those who attended them should not be disappointed, and for the same reason many imitators have arisen who have not even the excuse of some original mediumistic power. All mediums are therefore by their very nature subject to the greatest suspicion, those of them at least who are capable of producing objective phenomena, and even should they be of unimpeachable good faith they become entirely irresponsible when in a state of trance, and every precaution must be taken to ensure the elimination of actual physical action on their part.

The various forms of phenomena produced may be summed up as follows: the first stages of the progression being very common even among normal individuals, the later stages being extremely rare. The various stages give us a very clear notion of the gradual transition from sensitive but normal human beings to mediums of exceptional merit, and suggest that these powers are latent in a number of individuals and are only accidentally developed in some; in other words, although we can observe them when present, we have no means at present of controlling, awakening, or developing them.

In the first stage or degree the subject is not susceptible to hypnotism, but on being taken by the hand, and if he is asked to think of some object he has hidden in the room, he is much astonished when, guided by his unconscious movements, the operator discovers that object. In the second stage or degree the subject can be hypnotised. If we tell him he is really an old man, for instance, he will cough, spit, and generally act the part for hours at a time. In the third stage the subject falls into a trance through auto-suggestion, and imagining herself to be Marie Antoinette, for instance, will speak the language, write the hand, and use the spelling of the Queen of France.

In the fourth stage Mrs. Piper, to take a concrete example, gradually loses her normal consciousness, she is then controlled by exterior and mysterious personalities, most probably imaginary, but who are apparently gifted with extraordinary cryptesthesic faculties. As an example of the fifth stage, Eusapia Palladino falls into a trance, and through the intermediate action of the mysterious entity or being she calls John King, she causes heavy objects to move and remain suspended in mid-air, or materialises hands, heads, or complete human forms.

We may more briefly call mediums those who produce objective phenomena, sensitive beings those who are gifted with the faculty of cryptesthesis, and automatons those who quite unconsciously produce such phenomena as automatic writing.

It is sometimes difficult to distinguish between merely psychic phenomena and metapsychic phenomena. Richet uses the following definition. 'Any phenomenon which can be produced by human intelligence is psychic, any phenomenon which cannot be produced by the human intelligence, however deep and subtle, is metapsychic.'

For instance, Helen Smith writes and speaks fluent Sanscrit without having ever read or learned or heard any word of Sanscrit. This is a metapsychic phenomenon.

A certain person in a form of trance writes with great rapidity excellent poetry, absolutely perfect both as regards style and form. This is purely psychic, for some people can write excellent verses rapidly, and therefore perhaps also this particular person under certain special conditions, and, moreover, the necessary knowledge and material for their production is present.

Of course, in the observation of all such phenomena the question of probability must be very carefully considered. For instance, I ask a person, 'What was the name of the person who wrote to me this morning?' and he answers, 'Mary,' and in fact the letter was signed 'Lucy'; but suddenly I remember that I did in fact receive another letter that morning signed 'Mary' which I was not thinking of at the time. At first sight the very error makes the case appear more extraordinary and conclusive; but in reality this is not so. To begin with, two answers were possible, 'Mary' and 'Lucy,' so that the probabilities of a correct answer are really twice as great. A great deal of attention must be paid to points of this nature if any conclusion is to be drawn from observations.

As far as normal people are concerned experiments in telepathy have been carried out times without number, but serious experiments on this subject are few and far between.

Recent experiments carried out by means of broadcasting were entirely inconclusive. The reason for this is fairly obvious. A long period of training is necessary before any operator can really 'make his mind a blank' or get into the true receptive state, and the same is true of concentration at the transmitting end. The slightest interruption is fatal, and under the circumstances it is small wonder that the results obtained were nil.

In a similar experiment carried out by M. Kerdman, a professor at Cambridge University, the results obtained were as follows: –

Object thought of	Answer given
Red	Red
Golden	Yellow
R	R
E	E
Isosceles triangle	Right-angle triangle
Pyramids of Egypt	Tetrahedron
Five of clubs	Five of spades

The results are very conclusive. In some very good experiments carried out by F. L. Usher and Burt (A.S.P. 1910.20.14-21, 40-45) over two distances, Bristol to London and Praga to London, the results were as follows. The experiments were on cards. There were sixty experiments altogether.

Long distance	Entirely correct	4	Probability	1.1
	Value correct	14	'	4.5
	Colour correct	28	'	30
Short distance	Entirely correct	9	'	0.7
	Value correct	15	'	2.7
	Colour correct	20	'	18

These experiments are chosen as typical of a great number of similar results, and show that even in normal human beings such a thing as cryptesthesis exists. What the mental process is we do not know. These phenomena, as might be expected, are much more marked in cases of hypnotism and mediumistic trance, and in such cases telepathy can no longer explain the facts. In many of these experiments, in order to eliminate the possibility of telepathy, no person present knows what the object to be guessed is, and yet these objects are correctly described as though 'seen' by the medium.

The following experiments conducted in Warsaw by Professor Richet and Doctor Geley are very remarkable. The medium was M. O.

(1) A sealed letter, the contents of which are unknown to anyone, is handed to the medium. He says, 'It is short, a few words, good wishes for Poland, no signature.' The envelope contained the words 'Good wishes for your success in Warsaw.'

(2) Another sealed envelope, same conditions. He says, 'Ideas from Pascal, Man is weak, a weak reed, a reed that thinks.' The letter contained the following quotation from Pascal, 'Man is a reed, the weakest reed in nature, but a reed that thinks.'

(3) Another sealed letter, same conditions. He says, 'What a chaos. What connection can there be between fish and Poland, Long live Poland.' The envelope contained (a) drawings of camels, (b) the following words: 'a peal of bells,' 'a fish,' 'Long live Poland.'

(4) A piece of paper had been previously enclosed in a leaden tube with walls half an inch thick and the tube was sealed. No one knew what the contents of the tube might be since it had been drawn at random from many others. It actually contained the drawing of a man in chauffeur's cap and coat, the face being left blank with the exception of a very heavy moustache. The medium said, ' A drawing, a man with a big moustache. He is dressed in military uniform. He resembles Pilsudski. He is fearless, he is like a knight.' The latter part of the description refers to the fact that across the drawing the words 'Un chevalier sans peur et sans reproche' had been written. The astonishing description of what was really a most unusual object is a striking example of the wonderful accuracy of some of the results obtained.

Cases of monitions abound in everyday life, so many examples of these have been given that it would be really superfluous to quote any here. Cases when people were actually seen or heard in places where they could not possibly have been at the time are common and appear to be caused by the intense desire to communicate some sort of information or sometimes a warning to some friend or parent, but quite often they are due to some futile preoccupation usually intensified by a delirious state. Whether these apparitions are objective in the true sense of the word it is very difficult to say, but in a number of cases they have been seen and heard by several people, either separately or collected together, and even by animals, although this is no proof of their objectivity and points rather to the phenomenon known as collective hallucination.

Whatever we may call it, the fact remains that these occurrences are real, frequent, authentic, and quite impossible to explain. Curious though these phenomena may be, premonition, or the knowledge of a fact which has not yet occurred, is far more difficult to understand. One example of this is so precise in detail, so extraordinary, and the accident so unusual that it carries conviction in itself, although cases of similar phenomena are numerous. The lady in question was in point of fact Professor Richet's mother, and the lady to whom the accident was revealed by a medium long before its occurrence her niece. The niece met, at a friend's house in April 1884, and quite by accident, a person gifted with mediumistic faculties who immediately said to her, 'Someone closely connected with you is about to be the victim of a horrible accident.' The lady answered, 'Is it my mother?' and the person answered, 'No, it is a person closely connected with you, and she will he crushed by a wall' On the 7th of June, 1884, the aunt of the lady in question, and mother of Professor Richet, was crushed to death by the wall of a dam, the sudden collapse of which buried her under the debris. This case is in itself so strange and so perfect that it is hardly necessary to add another. The unusual nature of the accident makes it absolutely unique.

In dealing with telekinesis, the only experiments which can be considered as convincing are those in which no contact whatsoever exists between the medium and the object moved. It is too difficult to eliminate the possibility of muscular action whenever there is contact, however slight, to make such experiments really reliable. Here again good examples of telekinesis are fairly numerous. I have chosen a few typical cases.

Here is one due to Home and observed by Mr. Valery, chief engineer of the Transatlantic and International Telegraph Companies.

'In my own house, where Home had never been, and seven feet behind his back, stood a small table. Home was sitting on a chair, I was holding his hands, and both his legs lay across my knees. There was light in the room. Suddenly the table began to move, it came rapidly towards me, and a huge sofa, large enough to hold eight people, was moved bodily across the room. The whole time I was holding Home's hands and feet, and fraud was out of the question.' During another experiment with Home, observed by Sir William Crookes, a heavy dining-room table was lifted off the ground, a foot and a half clear, in broad daylight, while Crookes actually held both Home's feet and hands.

During experiments carried out by Eusapia Palladino she appears to exert great muscular effort, her muscles contract, and she moves as though she was actually putting forth the necessary muscular strength to produce the movement, although there is, of course, no contact whatsoever.

Eusapia was in all cases elaborately searched, she wore tights, and the room was absolutely bare, beyond the presence of a chair or table and a curtain. There was often a subdued light in the room.

This question of darkness has often been used as an argument to support the theory that all spiritualistic phenomena were necessarily fraudulent since they could not be otherwise produced. This idea is absurd, since in the present state of our knowledge we do not and cannot say whether or not darkness is an essential requirement. It would be just as absurd to ask a photographer to develop a plate in broad daylight and accuse him of fraud should he refuse or be unable to do so.

As regards ectoplasmia, or actual materialisation, I will describe at some length an extraordinary experiment which is probably one of the most conclusive ever made. The medium was Frank Kluski and the observers were Doctor Geley and Professor Richet. During the experiments (1) both of Kluski's hands were strongly and continually held; (2) no other person could possibly enter the room; (3) no movement of any kind was permitted, either on the part of the medium or of the assistants; (4) the light was sufficient to perceive any motion.

The mouldings which I am about to describe were obtained by the use of a bath of molten paraffin wax, at a temperature of 43 degrees C., into which it was required that the materialised object should be plunged. On being removed, a hand, for instance, would be naturally covered with a thin coating of wax which would solidify as it cooled. Now on dematerialisation taking place – the truly extraordinary feature of these experiments – the hand or object disappears from within these mouldings, which are left behind. If we suppose that Kluski, or even a confederate, could possibly have themselves plunged their hands into the wax (and the noise of the splashing was distinct) it would, of course, be materially impossible for them to remove the wax 'glove' thus formed, even more so from a foot, without destroying it. In fact in one case the fingers of the hand are clenched. It is impossible from the very nature of the mouldings and the clear impressions of the slightest pores, veins, and ridges to suppose that they should have been produced by inflated rubber formers, which, anyway, the medium could not have hidden about his person, on account of the particularly severe searching to which he was subjected. Besides, the wax moulds are so fragile that such an operation would have been impossible.

Richet and Geley had taken the precaution of introducing a colourless chemical into the wax in order that this might be afterwards identified and ensure that the mouldings were made in the room and at the time of the seance.

Although some of the cases given by Professor Richet relating to materialisations and apparitions are very remarkable and of extraordinary interest, we feel that the above experiment, though less spectacular, constitutes a most convincing and beautifully simple demonstration. Feet and hands were repeatedly produced in this fashion, and a set of plaster casts made from the wax are, at the time of writing, on view at the Psychic Museum, Victoria Street, Westminster, S.W.1.

We may therefore conclude by accepting the reality of three distinct types of phenomena: Cryptesthesis, which is fairly common; Telekinesis, which is rarer; and Ectoplasmia or materialisation, which is the rarest of all. The amount of evidence collected, the extraordinary pains taken to avoid even unconscious fraud, the fact that all the assistants concerned were scientific men of considerable repute and free from any mystic or religious bias, are facts which leave us very little room for doubt. I must refer the reader to Richet's work, wherein he will find a wealth of information and the exact accounts of innumerable other experiments. My object has only been to give the reader a definition of the science, of the facts on which it is based, and the main headings under which its various manifestations can be grouped.

The sole remaining apparently supernatural phenomena to be found in the lore of the past are really identical with the facts of modern metapsychics, after the modifications due to the time which has elapsed and the exaggerations and fancies of recorders have been allowed for. Whether the true initiates of remote initiations knew the explanation of such phenomena, or were able to develop and control them at will, is a secret to which we have no clue. We must be grateful to the patient investigators who have worked, and are still working, on the subject for the results obtained, and for the sober outlook they have adopted in this connection. Let us remember that the scales of Lavoisier did more for the cause of chemistry than the countless volumes of alchemy, and after all, as the Bible has it, 'Omnia in numero et pondera.'

BIBLIOGRAPHY

Aban, P. Les oeuvres magiques de C. Agrippa. (Grimoire.)

Abhedananda, Swami. Divine Heritage of Man. New York, 1903.

Abhedananda, Swami. How to be a Yogi. New York, 1902.

Abhedananda, Swami. India and her People. New York, 1906.

Agrippa, Cornelius. De Occulta Philosopha. 1651.

Albertus Magnus. Compositum de Compositis. 1890.

Albertus Magnus. De Mineralibus. 1518.

Albigeois. Deux livres de la raison, par Louis de Santi et Auguste

Vidal. Paris, 1896.

Allemagne, H. R. d'. Les Cartes b. jouer du XIVe au XXe siecles. Paris, Hachette.

Alviella, Comte d'. The Migration of Symbols. London, 1894.

Alviella, Comte d'. Introduction à l'histoire generale des religions.

Alviella, Comte d'. Croyances, rites et institutions. Paris, 1911.

Amelineau, E, Les idées sur Dieu dans l'ancienne Egypte. Paris, 1893.

Archaic rock inscriptions (Phallic). Anonymous.

Atkinson, W. The Inner Consciousness. Chicago, Masonic Temple, 1908.

Atkinson, W. The Law of the New Thought. London, 1902.

Baissac, Jules. Les Grands Jours de la Sorcellerie. Paris, 1890.

Barlet, F. C. Les Genies planetaires. Paris, 1921.

Barrès. Un renovateur de l'occultisme. Paris, 1898.

Barrett, Francis. The Magus. London, 1801.

Baudoin. Psychologic de la suggestion. Paris, 1922.

Baudot, Jaques. Les visions de Jacques Baudot. Paris, 1802.

Beauchamp, Jeanne. Etudes comparées de la doctrine Esoterique des religions et philosophies religieuses. Paris, 1912.

Béliard. Les Sorciers, reveurs et demoniaques. Paris, 1920.

Berbiguier. Les Farfadets. Paris, 1821.

Bernard. La Revelation. Etudes sur les Religions comparées. Paris, 1911.

Bernheim. De la suggestion. Paris.

Bersot. Du Spiritualisme et de la nature. Paris, 1846.

Berthelot, M. P. E. Les origines de l'Alchimie. Paris, 1885.

Bertrand, Abbé. Les stances de Haidari. Recits historiques et élégiaques sur la vie et la mort des principaux martyrs musulmans. Paris, 1845.

Besant, A. Les trois senders. Paris, 1924.

Bhagavad-Gita. Paris, 1922.

Bhagavad-Gita, compiled by Yogi Ramacharaka. Chicago, 1907.

Bibliotheca Diabolica Bibliography. Anonymous, 1874.

Bilz, F. E. La nouvelle Medication Naturelle. Paris.

Blanc, H. Le Merveilleux dans le Jansinisme, Le Magnetisme, le Méthodisme, et le Baptiste Americains, Tepidemie de Morzine, le Spiritisme. Paris, 1865.

Blavatsky, H. P. Les origines du Rituel dans TEglise et dans la Mafonnerie. Paris.

Bcehme, Jacob. See Boutroux, E.

Bois, J. Le Satanisme et la Magic. Paris, 1897.

Bose, J. Chunder. Response in the Living and Non-Living. London: Longmans, 1902.

Box, Ernest. Belisama ou l'Occultisme Celtique. Paris, 1910.

Bouché Leclercq. Histoire de la divination (2 vols.). Paris, 1882.

Bouché Leclerq. L'Astrologie Greque. Paris, 1899.

Bourgeat, J. G. La Magie. Paris, 1909.

Bourgeat, J. G. Rituel de Magie divine. Paris, 1914.

Boutroux, E. Le Philosophe Allemand Jacob Boehme. Paris, 1888.

Bovet, de. Histoire des dernier Pharaons et des premiers Rois de Perse. Avignon, 1835.

Bovier de Fontenelle. Histoire des Oracles. Paris, 1908.

Britt, Ernest Gamme siderale et gamme musicale. Paris, 1924.

Broc, P. P. Essai sur les races humaines. Paris, 1836.

Brucker, History of Philosophy. London.

Cahagnet, L. A. Magie magnétique. Paris, 1858.

Caillet, A. I. Manuel bibliographique des Sciences Psychiques ou Occultes. Paris: Porbon, 1913.

Callet, Auguste. L'Enfer. Paris, 1861.

Calmet, Don Augustin. Dissertation sur les Vampires de Hongrie, etc. Paris, 1766.

Campbell, J. G. Witchcraft and Second Sight in the Highlands and Islands of Scotland. Glasgow, 1902.

Carbonarisne. Mémoires by Rufini. Paris, 1855.

Chabouillet. Catalogue raisonné des Camdes et pierres de la bibliotheque imperiale. Paris, 1858.

Clavicules de Salomon. Paris; Daragon, 1914.

Clodd, E. Animism. London: Constables.

Cooper-Oakley, I. Mystical Traditions. Milan: Ars Regia, 1909.

Coutance, A. Empoisonneurs, Empoisonnes, Venins et poisons. Paris: Rothschild, 1888.

Cultus Arborum. Anonymous.

Curzon, H. de. La Regie du Temple. Paris, 1886.

Dadachangi, R. K. Origin of Circumcision and Idol Worship.

Davenport. Aphrodisiacs and Anti-aphrodisiacs.

Davenport. Curiositatis Eroticae Physiologiae.

Davis, Jackson. The Approaching Crisis, being a review of Dr. Bushnell's recent lectures on Supernaturalism. New York, 1852.

Déterminisme Astral. Paris: Bodin, 1905.

Dresser, H. W. Hegel, the Philosophy of the Spirit. London, 1908.

Druids, complete history of. London, 1894.

Dubois, J. A. Moeurs, institutions et ceremonies des peuples de Plnde. Paris, 1825.

Dulaure, Jaques Antoine. Des cultes qui ont precedes et amenés l'idolatrie. Paris, 1805.

Dulaure, Jaques Antoine. Des divinites génératrices. Paris, 1885.

Dulora de la Hage. Somnambulisme et Magie. Paris, 1896.

Dumoutier, G. Les symbols, les emblemes du cuke chez les Anamites. Paris, 1891.

Du Potet. Cours de magnetisme animal. Paris, 1834.

Du Potet, Baron. La Magic devoilee, Paris, 1907.

Durville, H. Le Fantome des Vivants. Paris, 1909.

Durville, Henri. Congres International de Psychologie Expérimentale. Paris, 1910.

Durville, Henri. La science secrete. Paris.

Eckhartshausen, D'. La Nude sur Ie Sanctuaire. Paris, Muséum Hermeticum.

Eliphas Levi. The Magical Ritual of the Sanctum Regnum Interpreted by the Tarot. London, 1896.

Eliphas Levi. La Clef des Grands Mysteres. Paris, 1861.

Eliphas Levi. Clefs Majeures et Clavicules de Salomon. Paris, 1895.

Eliphas Levi. Histoire de la Magie. Paris, 1860.

Eliphas Levi. Dogme et rituel de la Haute Magie. Paris.

Eliphas Levi. Traité des esprits. Paris.

Eliphas Levi. Le Grand Arcane. Paris.

Eliphas Levi. Unpublished Writings. The Paradoxes of Highest Science. Theosophical Miscellanies. Calcutta, 1883.

Enchiridion. Physicae restitutae, tractatus Arcanum Hermeticae philosophiae opus. Paris, 1642.

Ennemoser, Joseph. History of Magic. London, 1854.

Erdan, Alex. La France Mystique. Tableau des excentricités religieuses de ce temps. Amsterdam, Meslier, 1858.

Famin, César. Musée Royal de Naples, le Cabinet secret. Editeur Palais Royal, 2 et 3 Galerie des Chartes.

Faye, E. de. Gnostiques et Gnosticisme. Paris, 1925.

Fehlinger. Sexual Life of Primitive People. London, 1921.

Figuier, Louis. L'Alchimie et les Alchimistes. Paris, 1856.

Figuier, Louis. Physiologic Universelle. Le secret d'Hermés. Paris, 1872.

Fire, Fishes and Flowers (Phallic). Anonymous.

Fishes, Fire and Flowers (Phallic). Anonymous.

Flagellation, History of. Anonymous.

Flers, de H. Des hypothbes. Gnose synthetique. Paris, 1899.

Flowers, Fishes and Fire (Phallic). Anonymous.

Fludd, R. Etude du Macrocosme. Paris, 1907.

Fontane, M. Histoire Universelle. Les Iranians, Zoroastre. Paris, 1881.

Fontenelle, Bovier de. Histoire des Oracles. Paris, 1908.

Forlong, J. G. R. Faiths of Man (3 vols.) London, 1906.

Forlong, J. G. R. Short Studies in Science. London, 1897.

Forlong, J. G. R. Studies in Comparative Religion.

Forlong, J. G. R. The Rivers of Life. London, 1883.

Fowler, W. W. The Roman Festivals. London, 1899

Frazer, Doctor. The Golden Bough. London, 1911.

Gabalis, Comte de, or The Extravagant Mysteries of the Cabalists. London.

Gaffarel, j. Profonds mysteres de la Cabale Divine. Paris, 1912.

Geley, Gustave, Dr. La Physiologic dite supra-normale et les phénomènes d'Idioplastie. Paris, 1918.

Gombault, Abbé. Les apparitions de Tilly-sur-Seuilles. Paris, 1896.

Groot, J. J. M. The Religious System of China. Leyden, 1907.

Guaita, Stanilas de. Essai des Sciences Mandites (2 vols.). Paris.

Guldenstubbe, L. de. Pneumatologie positive. Paris, 1873.

Gyr, l'Abbé. La Franc Maçonnerie en elle-meme. Liege, Paris, 1859.

Haatan, A. Contribution à l'etude de PAlchimic. Paris, 1905.

Haddon, A. C. Magic and Fetishism. London, Constables.

Haiyam, Jabir ibu, de Alchimia libri tres. 1531.

Hancarville, P. F. H. Antiquites Etrusques, Greques et Romaines. Paris, 1785.

Hannay. Sex Symbolism in Religion. London, 1922

Hannay. The Roman Religion, its Rise and Decline. London.

Harris, Rendel. Origin of Apple Cults.

Harris, Rendel. Origin of Cult of Aphrodite.

Hartzheim, R. P. Gasp. Explicatio Fabularum et Superstitionum, quarum in S. Scripturis fit mcntio; vario hinc inde sensu praeter literalem, ut allegorico, morali, anagogico, etc. Colonioe Aggripinoe, 1724.

Hashnu, Kara O. Concentration and the Acquirement of Personal Magnetism. Fowler, 1906.

Havelock Ellis. The Psychology of Sex. London.

Hegel, G. W. F. Lectures on the Philosophy of Religion. Translation by Spiers and Sanderson. London, 1877.

Hegel, G. W. F. The Mystical Element in Hegel's Early Theological Writings, London, 1910.

Hegel, G. W. F. The Origin and Significance of Hegel's Logic. London, 1901.

Heindel, Mase. The Rosicrucian Cosmo-Conccption. London, Fowler.

Hermetic Art. A Short Enquiry. Anonymous, 1893.

Hermetic Dictionary. Anonymous, 1695.

Hermetis Trismagisti. Tabula Smaragdina vindicata per W. C. Kreigsmanum. 1657.

Hesart de la Villemarqué. La legende Celtique et la poesie des Cloitres en Irlande, en Cambric, et en Bretagne. Paris, 1864.

Higgins, Frank Charles. The Cross of the Magi. 1912.

History of Flagellation. Anonymous.

Hobhouse, L. T. Morals in Evolution. London: Chapman and Hall.

Hodgson. Essais on the language, litterature and religion of Nepal and Tibet. London, 1874.

Holdich, Sir T. Tibet the Mysterious. London, 1906.

Huysmans, J. K. Lk bas. Paris, 1891.

Inman, Thomas. Ancient Faiths. London, 1868.

Inman, Thomas. Ancient Pagan and Modern Symbolism. London, 1869.

International Catalogue of Scientific Literature. Anthropology. London Royal Society.

Jabir ibu Haiyam, de Alchimia libri tres. 1531.

Jagot, P. C. Methode Scientifique Moderne de Magnetisme, Hypnotisme. Suggestion. Paris, 1925.

Jennings, Hargrave. Illustrations of Phallism. 1887. Published, George Redway, 15 York Street.

Jesuites History, etc., by J, Cretineau-Joly. Paris, 1846.

Jhounet, a. Esoterisme et Socialisme. Paris, 1893.

Jollivet, Castelot F. La Science Alchimique. Paris, 1904.

Juillot de la Morrandière. Hermes et Toeuvre d'Homere. Paris, 1917.

Julien l'Apostat. OEuvres completes. Paris: Plon, 1863.

Khunrath, H. Amphitheatrum. 1609 edition.

King, C. W. Gnostics and their Remains. London, 1887.

Kircher, Athanasius. De Lapide Philosophorum. Roma, 1702.

Kircher, Athanasius. Latium. Amstelodami, 1671.

Kircher, Athanasius. Oedipus Aegypticus: hoc est Universalis Hieroglyphics veterum doctrine temporum injuria abolitis instauratio. Roma, 1652.

Knight, Payne. The Worship of Priapus. London, 1865.

Lancelin, Charles. Histoire Mythique de Shatan. Paris, 1903.

Lancelin, Charles. La sorcellerie des campagnes. Paris.

Lancelin, Charles. Le Ternaire Magique de Shatan. Paris, 1903.

Lang, A. The Totem Taboo and Exogamy. Man. No. 87.

La Saussaye, L. de. Dissertation sur le lieu de l'assemblée annuelle des Druides. Paris, 1864.

Laurence Dr. W. The sacred book of death of Hindu Spiritism; Soul transition and Reincarnation. Chicago, 1907.

Layard. Nineveh and its Remains. London.

Lecanu, Abbé. Histoire de Satan. Paris, 1861.

Leclerq, Bouché. Histoire de la divination (2 vols.). Paris, 1882.

Leclerq, Bouché. L'Astrologie Grecque. Paris, 1899.

Legge, J. Sacred Books of the East, Vol. 16, Part 2. Yih-Ching.

Legge, J. The Religions of China. London, 1880,

Légué, Dr. G. La Messe Noire. Paris, 1903.

Leibnitz. Ossum Hanoveranum sive miscellanae ex ore et schedis illustris viri piae memoriae Godofr. Guilielmi Leibnitz, etc. Lipsiae, J. Chr. Martini, 1718.

Lemne, Tevin. De Miraculis Occultis Naturae. Francofurti, 1640.

Lenain. La science Cabalistique, reprint of 1823 edition. Paris.

Lenglet-Dufresnoy, Alli. Histoire de la philosophie Hermétique. Paris, 1842.

Lenormand, Francois. Les Sciences occultes en Asie. Paris, 1875.

Lenormand, Francois. La divination chez les Chaldeens. Paris.

Lenormant, Jean. Histoire Veritable, etc. Paris, 1623.

Livre des mystères du Ciel et de la terre. Translated from Ethiopian by J. Perrochon. Paris, 1903.

Loève-Veimars, A. Precis de l'histoire des tribunaux secrets dans le Nord de l'Allemagne. Paris: Carez, 1824.

Lofthouse, W. F. Mithology and Monotheism. London: Quarterly Review, 1906, 301-3 19.

London, P. Lhasa. London, 1905.

Lulli, Raymond. Fasciculus Aureus. 1630.

Lulli, Raymond. La Clavicule. 1647.

MacClatchie, Thomas. Confutian Cosmogony. London, 1874.

Mackay. Popular Delusions. London.

Mackay. The Symbolism of Freemasonry. London.

Maillard de Chambure. Règles et statuts secrets des Templiers. Paris, 1840.

Malefices et Sorciers. Lille: Lelen, 1862.

Manava Dharma Castra. Paris, 1893.

Marconis, J. Et, Travaux complets des Sublimes Maitres du Grand oeuvre. Paris, 1866.

Marriage Ceremonies and Priapic Rites. Anonymous.

Masculine Cross. Anonymous.

Menant, Joachim. Les Yesidis. Annales du Musee Guimet. Paris, 1892.

Modène, Léon de. Ceremonies et coutumes qui s'observent aujourd'hui parmi les Juifs, etc. Lyon: Comba, 1684.

Moir, George. Magic and Witchcraft. London, 1852.

Morienus Romanus. Liber de Compositione Alchemicse. 1702.

Murray, Margaret Alice. The Witch Cult. London, 1921.

Musee Royal de Naples. Le Cabinet secret. Famin, Cesar, Editeu Palais Royal. Galerie des Chartes. 1857.

Mysteries of the Rosy Cross. Anonymous. London, 1891.

Narawainsyami Aiyer. Yoga Vaschista. Madras, 1896.

Nature worship. Anonymous.

Olechnowitz. Dr. Esquisse d'une histoire de la civilisation de l'humanité d'apres la methode brahmanique. Paris, 1882.

Olivet, Fabre d'. La langue Hebraique restituee. Paris.

Olivet, Fabre d'. Essais philosophiqucs sur le genre humain. Paris.

Oman, J. C. Cults, Customs, and Superstitions of India. London, 1908.

Ophiolatreia. Anonymous.

Papus. La pierre philosophale.

Papus. Le Tarot des Bohemiens. London, 1896.

Papus. Traite Elementaire de Magie Pratique. Paris

Patandyali. Yoga sastra. Paris, 1914.

Paw, C. de. Recherches philosophiques sur les Egyptiens et les Chinois. Amsterdam, 1773.

Péladan, Sar. Amphitheatre des Sciences Mortes, V, L'Occulte Catholique. Paris, 1899.

Phallic Miscellanies. Anonymous.

Phallic Objects and Remains. Anonymous.

Phallic Worship. Anonymous.

Phallism. Anonymous.

Pitt-Rivers, General. Evolution of Culture. Oxford: Clarendon Press.

Plato. Omnia divini Platonis Opera. Basilae, in officina Frolentiana. 1532.

Pluquet. Dictionnaire des Heresies, des erreurs, et des schisms. Paris, 1847.

Plutarque. Isis et Osiris. Paris, 1924.

Plytoff, G. La magie. Paris, 1892.

Plytoff, G. Les sciences occultes. Paris, 1891.

Priapic Rites and Marriage Ceremonies. Anonymous.

Priapus, worship of. Payne Knight. B.M. sec P.C. I9.a.2.

Quincey. Rosicrucianism and Freemasonry. London.

Ragon, J. M. La messe et ses mysteres. Paris, 1882.

Ramacharaka. Gnani Yoga. Chicago, 1907.

Ramacharaka. Hatha Yogi. Chicago, 1905.

Ramacharaka. The Hindu-Yogi Science of Breath. Chicago, 1905.

Ramacharaka The Inner Teachings of the Philosophies and Religions of India. Chicago, 1906.

Ramacharaka. Raja Yoga. Chicago, 1906.

Regis, E. Precis de psychiatric. Paris, 1914.

Reinach, S. L'Art et la Magie. Paris.

Rendel Harris. Origin of Apple Cults.

Rendel Harris. Origin of Cult of Aphrodite

Reymond, Dr. H. C. Physiologic et Evolution de I'amour sexuel à travers les ages et les races humaines. Paris, librairie des publications artistiques. (No date.)

Richet, Charles. Traite de Metapsychique. Paris, 1923.

Rolle, P. N. Recherches sur le cuke de Bacchus. Paris, 1824.

Rosy-Cross . Anonymous.

Roure, P. Lucien. Au pays de Poccultisme. Paris, 1925.

Santini de Riols. Les parfums magiques. Paris, 1903.

Santini DE Riols. Les picrres magiques. Paris, 1905.

Schemani. Magie et Magnctismc. Paris, 1925.

Schemani. Divination. Paris, 1925.

Schertz, Charles Ferdinand. Magia postuma. Olmutz, 1706.

Schopenhauer. Will and Idea. Translated by Haldane and
Kemp. London, 1883.

Sciences mysterieuscs. Paris: Deslinecrcs, 1899.

Sédir. Initiations. Rouen, 1924.

Sepher letzirah. Translation by Ctessc Calomira de Cimara.
Paris, 1913.

Sinnett, A. P. Esoteric Buddhism. London, 1883.

Sinnett, A. P. Collected Fruits of Occult Teaching. London,
1919.

Skeat, W. W. Malay Magic. London, 1900.

Stanislas, Julien. Le livre des recompenses et des peines
traduit du Chinois. Paris, 1835.

Swedenburg. The Heavenly Secrets. London, 1862.

Talmud, from Daniel Bomberg text, Venice, 1520. Arranged
by Jean de Pauly. Orleans, 1900.

Taylor, T. Eleusinian Mysteries. London, 1790.

Teissier, C. A. Manuel General de Maçonnerie. Paris, 1883.

Thorpe. Ancient Laws and Institutes of England. London,

1840.

This, Placido de. Physiomathematica sive Coelestis Philosophia. Mediolani, 1650.

Trismosion, Salomon. Splendor Solis. Alchemical treatises of Salomon Trismosion, adept and teacher of Paracelsus, etc. London: Kegan Paul, 1922.

Trithème, Jean. Traitc des Qauses Secondes. Paris, 1897.

Van Helmont, J. B. Ortus Medicinae id est initia Physical inaudita, etc. Lugdini: J. B. Devenet, 1655.

Vesper, Noel. Le Sens et l'Esprit de la terre. Lourmarin, 1925.

Villeneuve-Bargemont. Templiers, Monumens des Grands Maitres. Paris, 1829.

Vincent, F. V. De Tldolatrie chez les Anciens et les Modernes. Paris, 1850.

Vivekananda, Swami. The East and the West. Madras, 1909.

Vivekanamda, Swami. Inspired Talks. Madras.

Vivekananda, Swami. Juana Yoga. New York.

Vivekananda, Swami. Karma Yoga. New York, 1901.

Vivekananda, Swami. Raja Yoga, also Patandjali's Yoga aphorisms. New York, 1899.

Waddell, L. A. Tibet and Buddhism, or Lamaism. London, 1895.

Waddell, L. A. Thasa and its Mysteries. London, 1905.

Wake, C. S. Serpent Worship. London, 1888.

Wake and Westropp. Ancient Symbol Worship.

Westcott, Dr. W. W. Numbers, their Occult Power and Mystic Virtues. London, 1890.

Westcott, Dr. W. W. The Kaballah. London, 1910.

Westcott, Dr. W. W. Sepher Yetzirah. London, 1893.

Westropp. Ancient Symbol Worship. London, 1874.

Westropp. Primitive Symbolism. London, 1885.

Westropp and Wake. Ancient Symbol Worship.

Wirth, Oswald. The Book of Thoth.

Yogandranathra Bhattachava. Hindu Casts and Sects. Calcutta, 1896.

Yogavachara. 1916.

Yoga vaschista. K. Narawanisyani Aiyer. Madras, 1896.

Yogesa-Chandra-Sastin. a handbook of Hindu pantheism. 1900.

Zaccone, Pierre. Histoire des Sociétés secrètes. Paris, 1879.

INDEX